RADICALS OR CONSERVATIVES?

AMERICAN POLITICS RESEARCH SERIES

RADICALS OR

CONSERVATIVES?

The Contemporary American Right

JAMES McEVOY III

UNIVERSITY OF CALIFORNIA, DAVIS
DEPARTMENT OF SOCIOLOGY

RAND MCNALLY & COMPANY · Chicago

AMERICAN POLITICS RESEARCH SERIES

Aaron Wildavsky, Series Editor

For

Robert Cooley Angell

and

Esther Yancey,

who encouraged me in this effort

and in many others

ACKNOWLEDGMENTS

THIS BOOK would not and could not have been written without the help of William A. Gamson and J. Merrill Shanks; my debts to them are immense and I want to acknowledge their help and encouragement throughout the project. Many of my colleagues and former professors have also made many important contributions to the book. Aaron Wildavsky, Nelson Polsby, Leon Mayhew, and Robert C. Angell all read and made many valuable comments on the manuscript. John F. Scott, Warren E. Miller, Philip E. Converse, Stuart A. Kanter, Jeffery M. Paige, Joe Lee Davis, John Higham, and Robert Athanasiou also helped me at crucial points in the project. Elizabeth McEvoy gave me invaluable encouragement and assistance throughout the writing of the book, and I am particularly grateful to her for her patience and wise counsel. I would also like to thank Mrs. Barbara Salazar of Rand McNally for her careful and beneficial editing of my text. None of these persons, of course, is responsible for any weakness or inadequacy in the following pages, but they are responsible for much that my readers may find worthwhile. I was fortunate to have their help.

Mrs. Lucy Dawidowicz and Mr. Milton Himmelfarb of the American Jewish Committee and the committee itself made possible, through their generous financial support, much of the data analysis. Grants from the International Business Machines Corporation, the Faculty Research Committee of the University of California at Davis, and the Horace H. Rackham School of Graduate Studies at the University of Michigan also helped support the study.

My research assistants, Mrs. Jennifer Campbell and Mr. Carl Nelson, and my typists, Miss Katherine Atkins and Mrs. Edna Jones, made contributions to this project that were, as any author (but perhaps not every reader) knows, absolutely crucial to the success of a project of this sort. My thanks to them.

vii

Acknowledgments

The staff of the Survey Research Center of the University of Michigan, through their election studies, collected and made available most of the data discussed here. Obviously, without their efforts a study such as this would not have been possible. I am grateful to the center and to Carolyn Geda for her help in securing these data.

Additionally, a survey conducted by Louis Harris Associates is discussed briefly in Chapter V. A description of that survey may be found in the reports of the Task Force on Political Assassination of the National Commission on the Causes and Prevention of Violence, for which I was a consultant to the Task Force on Political Assassination.

The analysis was performed at the computer centers at the University of Michigan and the University of California, Berkeley; I am grateful for the computer time that these centers made available to me for this project.

JAMES McEVOY III

Davis, California
June 1970

PREFACE

IN THE YEARS since the beginning of the New Deal a number of social movements and third parties have arisen in America to challenge the ruling coalitions of Democrats and Republicans. These challenges have come from both right and left; and with the rising prosperity of the nation, they have been increasingly motivated by values, styles, and symbols rather than by economic deprivation or discontent. A number of these movements and parties have been extremist, or perhaps more properly authoritarian, in the sense that they mobilized a substantial part of their support by explicit appeals that, if carried into action, would probably have resulted in the severe abridgment of the civil liberties of many persons and the violent repression of several unpopular minorities.

Among those groups of a rightist character I include the American Independent party, the Dixiecrats, William Dudley Pelley's Silver Shirts, the fascist movements led by Lawrence Dennis and Seward Collins, and the Union party (National Union for Social Justice), led by Father Charles Coughlin, William Lemke, and Francis Townsend. Another prominent group with authoritarian and racist overtones was the Share-the-Wealth program of "Kingfish" Huey P. Long, eventually inherited by Gerald L. K. Smith, who tried to form a coalition with the Union party in the election of 1936.

Altogether, these groups had little success at the polls. Although the strongest of them, the American Independent party, attained 13 percent of the vote for president in 1968 and at one point seemed fairly close to throwing the election into the House of Representatives, the evidence suggests that it cannot be credited with having shifted the victory from Humphrey to Nixon. It does, however, seem fair to say that its presence on the ballot in 1968 exerted considerable restraint on the two major parties' pronouncements about civil rights, and it appears to have influenced the choice (a second choice) of Spiro

Agnew as Richard Nixon's vice-president. There are many other examples of accommodation to a third party's presence by the major parties; taken together, they demonstrate clearly that while unsuccessful at the presidential level, the third parties have not been entirely without effect.

A number of other important opposition movements formed in this period within the Republican party. With the exception of the activities of the late Senator Joseph R. McCarthy, these movements, while often conservative, were not pervasively authoritarian. Most notable were the unsuccessful challenges to the Republican leadership led by Robert A. Taft and forces backing General Douglas MacArthur. Most recently, of course, was the successful (from the standpoint of intraparty competition) challenge led by F. Clifton White, Barry Goldwater, and , midwestern and western conservative Republican political elites which resulted in Goldwater's nomination in 1964.

Major leftist movements, at least those led by Upton Sinclair and Henry Wallace, did not prosper in the political climate of the New Deal. The massive growth of the trade-union movement during the thirties undoubtedly had much to do with this relative weakness of the left in the United States, but of course Stalinism and the Moscow trials, the cold war and Korea, the expansion of welfare-state policies, and the growth of the economy also played important roles in the limitation of leftist and working-class dissent. Recently, with the formation of loose coalitions of black civil rights advocates and radical students, a small but serious opposition has developed on the left, some factions of which have adopted an authoritarian stance. The Black Muslims, the Student Nonviolent (now National) Coordinating Committee, and some chapters of Students for a Democratic Society have taken positions that are often radically and violently intolerant of their adversaries.

The subject of this volume, however, is the American right, and specifically two recent rightist movements that attempted to capture the presidency. The first of these, led by Barry Goldwater, is by and large representative of the nonauthoritarian intraparty strain of rightist opposition movements; the other, led by George Wallace, represents a synthesis of populism with racism, and belongs within the tradition of authoritarian domestic movements that include those led by Long, Pelley, Coughlin, and Gerald L. K. Smith. It is important to recognize that despite the many and important differences between the Goldwater and Wallace movements, and, more generally, between the authoritarian and conservative traditions, there are also similarities so strong as to make comparison of these movements at least as appropriate as contrast. I have therefore started this study with an attempt to define rather specifically the ideological commonalities that bind these movements together in such a way as to make comparative analysis appropriate and, I hope, fruitful.

To say that Goldwater's supporters were conservative and that Wallace's candidacy was based on racist and populist appeals is not to say very much. While references to populism and classical American conservativism are useful in placing the movements in historical perspective, they can also be dangerous if we heed them so exclusively that our analysis becomes guided by historical precedent rather than contemporary fact. Furthermore, if we too often use value-laden terms such as "racist," "fascist," and "reactionary" in discussions of movements such as these, all we have gained is the approval of those who are willing to settle for simplistic, pejorative, and crude appraisals of what I believe are important and complex social and political phenomena.

Accordingly, I have made some fairly strenuous efforts to define the core beliefs of the American rightist elite and to show to what degree the supporters of this elite in the mass public are in fact motivated by the same kinds of concerns that are expressed by their leaders. Furthermore, from the beginning of this study, I have asked not how some groups could have supported a particular candidate, but rather why they did support him.

In my search for an understanding of the basic beliefs and ideology of contemporary rightist political movements, I have carefully read and analyzed numerous rightist and superpatriotic publications. Among the pervasive themes of these movements are intense nationalism, the need for severe restriction of the social welfare functions of government, concern for traditional morality, and intense anticommunism.

Is popular support for the American right expanding or contracting? An analysis of two selected indicators of this trend—public opinion polls and periodical circulation—proves somewhat inconclusive. I found both of them to be at least partially inadequate to the task of providing an answer to this question, but they are still the best indicators I could devise. Perhaps some reader will come forward with better ones for use in the future.

The research traditions of authoritarianism and mass-society theory form the background for much of the empirical work on the right that has been completed in the past few years. I have tried to state the premises of the theories that have been advanced to explain the right in a way sufficiently precise to permit the formulation of empirical statements from them, and have employed data from a number of studies as tests of the truth value of these statements.

An analysis of the demographic and class structure of the early supporters of Senator Goldwater in 1964—the people who favored him for the presidency prior to the Republican convention and who continued to support him after he won the nomination—lends insight into the contemporary American right, and calls into question the assumptions of some of Goldwater's critics that he and his followers were unsocialized political actors and/or had suffered some objective disruptions of their socioeconomic status locations. Data on the issue positions, policy preferences, level of political activity, and supposed political extremism of Goldwater's early supporters are drawn from the 1964 pre- and postelection studies of the University of Michigan's Survey Research Center.

A similar analysis of the supporters of George Wallace and the American Independent party in the election of 1968 should prove salutary to anyone who doubts that important differences existed between the Goldwater and Wallace movements.

Finally, I have proposed some ideas for my readers' consideration which I hope will be useful for development of a more comprehensive and credible theory of rightist political movements.

CONTENTS

LIST OF TABLES

LIST OF FIGURES

CHAPTER I

Is There a New
American Right?

AT THE MOST GENERAL level of consideration, the right can be thought
of as a social movement proposing the transformation of a particular
sociopolitical system into an imagined utopian state. In their extremes,
these changes are to be wrought only through the fundamental or
revolutionary alteration of the political and social structures that hap-
pen to prevail in the particular nation-state or in the international
political system that hosts such a revolutionary or radical social
movement.

As Cantril says:

A reasonable resolution of a conflict between a social movement and other
elements of society with which it may come into conflict is impossible
simply because the conflict is between two sets of assumptions or standards
of judgment. Any argument or reasoning of either side is bounded by these
assumptions. Hence, if the basic conditions giving rise to the conflicting
assumptions cannot be remedied before great numbers of people have
ardently and tenaciously accepted them, then, as history shows, the individuals who hold these conflicting values must try to get rid of each other.
What people live for they are willing to die for.[1]

When the structural conditions giving rise to the movement are
not sufficient to produce a large organized membership—a revolutionary
class—the movement is more than likely to engage in legitimate and

[1]Hadley Cantril, *The Psychology of Social Movements* (New York: Science
Editions, 1963), pp. 268–69.

1

quasi-legitimate political activity to further its cause. This is particularly evident in Western industrial nations with democratic political systems. In these societies there is a relatively greater potential for political responsiveness to the demands of a movement than is the case in the underdeveloped nations or in those countries unfortunate enough to be controlled by Soviet and Chinese Communist bureaucracies.

In contemporary America the large majority of rightist formal organizations have adopted this latter course. Only a few, like the Minutemen, the Ku Klux Klan, the American Nazi party, and some black militant and radical student groups openly espouse violence as a means of social change. In general, the right differs distinctively from other sociopolitical belief systems or ideologies in its emphasis on authority and intense nationalism, and often too in the fact that it sees its goal culture or utopia in the past rather than in the future.

"Right" is, of course, a relative term, and has had different meanings at different points in time and in different political contexts.[2] In America today, the right stresses the importance of states' rights or decentralized federalism, the role of individual responsibility for the maintenance of liberty, the importance of tradition and religion, the natural inequalities of men, and nationalism.[3] A seemingly contradictory integration of almost anarchistic individualism with a high level of approval of the two primary authoritarian institutions of American society—the military and the police—and the corollary of strong support for "law and order" characterize many of those who speak for the right today. Moreover, the fact that many formal rightist organizations and some members of the rightist segment of society perceive themselves as largely cut off from influence over the government may account for the fact that they almost completely deny legitimacy to one of the major political parties in the system and reject much of the legitimacy of the other.

The American right is procapitalist in economics and is, of course, strongly anticommunist. Especially among the more committed rightists, anticommunism is not merely confined to extranational communist

[2]See, for example, Seymour Martin Lipset, *Political Man* (New York: Double-day Anchor Books, 1963), chap. 5, pp. 127–79. The title of this chapter is "Fascism—Left, Right, and Center," and it examines at some length the various forms fascistic and rightist movements assume in various political cultures.

[3]See Clinton Rossiter, *Conservatism in America: The Thankless Persuasion,* rev. ed. (New York: Vintage Books, 1962), pp. 64–66, for a carefully constructed set of principles of conservatism as an American philosophical position. Many of these principles are given lip service by rightist ideologists, although their behavior often suggests a much more radical and revolutionary posture toward present and past social institutions.

objects, such as Cuba or the Soviet Union, but is focused primarily on what the organized right in America seems for the most part to present as its *raison d'être:* a major internal communist conspiracy, which under their definition often includes liberals, blacks, students, and others who dissent from the rightist position. In many of the publications and formal organizations of the American right, the theme of a general conspiracy is so evident as to warrant designation of this particular political position as a conspiracy theory of politics and history.[4] Finally, the spokesmen of the American right express strong concern for maintenance of the traditional forms of morality, which they believe to be disappearing from American life.

Limited government, a regionally dominant nationalism, militarism, patriotism, individual responsibility, militant anticommunism, and traditional morality are six major themes of concern and action that mobilize the opinion leaders and spokesmen of the contemporary right. These leaders' proposals for major structural change are centered on the dismantling or strict limitation of numerous agencies and social welfare policies of the federal government, with the exception of the military, and the establishment of a Jeffersonian-style federal system of relatively decentralized states. Implied also in some of the more militant rightist literature is an implementation of strict controls on free speech. The focus of much of the discontent that the American right voices in its publications is the Supreme Court, which has, of course, been the branch of the federal government most influential in the articulation of another Jeffersonian ideal—equality before the law—and which has, moreover, extended the application of the First Amendment to permit the free expression of views by communists and other unpopular persons, and has attempted as well to ameliorate the political and social disadvantages of blacks.

These few introductory remarks are by no means meant to imply that rightists themselves are a coherent or regimented social group organized around a shared ideological view of American political and social life, or that they form a revolutionary segment of the society. Although there are some persons who by affiliating with formal rightist organizations come to refine and perhaps adopt wholesale all the tenets of the American right, they are without question a tiny segment of the American population. Most of this discussion will not be concerned with such people, but rather with persons who may share certain views in common with the ideologues and ideologies of the right, but who have

[4]This idea is developed in great detail in William Chandler Baum, "The Conspiracy Theory of Politics of the Radical Right in the United States" (unpublished Ph.D. dissertation, Iowa State University, 1960).

probably not affiliated with any rightist voluntary association and whose beliefs are in most cases in less than total agreement and are certainly less constrained (i.e., logically ordered) than those of the rightist elite.

The contemporary *ideological* right is, of course, organized not simply around the propagation of an idealized goal culture; it is also concerned with the implications of this culture for interpretation of and response to present-day issues. An empirical determination of many of the salient issues of the elite or ideological segment of the American right has been made by Richard Schmuck and Mark Chesler,[5] and it will be useful to employ their descriptive categories of areas of concern to and issue positions advanced by those they have termed "super-patriots" to round out the description of the goal culture of the organized American right in the 1960s. Table I.1 shows that there is a high level of agreement among the rightist issue positions cited, the general areas of rightist concern into which the specific issues fit, and the even more general outline of rightist beliefs with which this chapter opened.

RIGHTIST POLITICAL ACTION

Extreme statements like the call for impeachment of President Eisenhower made by Robert Welch, the founder and leader of the John Birch Society, or the plot to gas members of the United Nations by the Minutemen, a paramilitary rightist group based in Missouri, are highly visible events but hardly the typical behaviors of most persons who affiliate with contemporary rightist organizations. More typical forms of political action by the members of these groups include soliciting signatures for petitions calling for the impeachment of former Chief Justice of the Supreme Court Earl Warren, organizing for the American Independent party, and working for the adoption of the "Liberty Amendment" to the Constitution, which would repeal the federal income tax. Members of rightist organizations also frequently participate in letter-writing campaigns directed at political elites, corporations, or governmental bodies, through which they attempt to influence the outcome of a particular piece of legislation or a corporate or governmental policy decision. One recent campaign, conducted in 1967 by a number of rightist organizations, sought to prevent passage of the treaty between the United States and the Soviet Union which established a system of consulates within the major cities of each of these nations. Other campaigns have centered on trying to secure American withdrawal from the United Nations, attacks on the patriotism

[5]Richard Schmuck and Mark Chesler, "On Super-Patriotism: A Definition and an Analysis," *Journal of Social Issues*, 19, no. 2 (April 1963): 31–50.

TABLE I.1

Some Superpatriot General Concerns and Specific Positions Advanced

Areas of Concern	Specific Positions Advanced
1. International political change and America's role	Against loss of national sovereignty Against threat of "enslavement" through international government Against cooperating with "evil" communist forces
2. Domestic political change and social equality	For states' rights Against egalitarianism Against using "biased" social science to form public policy
3. Economic changes in private and public enterprises	For free enterprise without governmental intervention Against trade with communist countries Against international trade agreements
4. Religious institutions and social change	Social service is not the mission of the church Not fighting against communism is sinful For a personalized church and religious system
5. Educational institutions and practice in change	Against permissiveness in schools For training in traditional moral values Against psychological counseling and testing, "brainwashing" and "brainpicking" Against federal influences in schools and curricula
6. Mental health of individuals	Against invasion of privacy Against use of psychology to analyze political activity Against permissiveness and impulse expression

Source: Richard Schmuck and Mark Chesler, "On Super-Patriotism: A Definition and an Analysis," *Journal of Social Issues,* 19, no. 2 (April 1963):34.

The table was constructed from a content analysis of superpatriotic literature published through 1962. Accordingly, some specific policy positions of superpatriot writers are not represented, in particular those arguing for further expansion of the war in Vietnam.

of various authors, and a spectacular assault on the Xerox Corporation for its sponsorship of a television series favorable to the United Nations. In that campaign, initiated by the John Birch Society, Xerox and its directors received more than twelve thousand protest letters.[6]

Other activities of American rightist groups include a "Support Your Local Police" campaign, a perennial effort at removing the United States from the United Nations and the United Nations from the United States, lobbying for a constitutional amendment allowing prayers and Bible-reading in the public schools, and, more recently, combating sex education courses in the schools and creating hundreds of front organizations whose purpose is to articulate the rightist position on any given current event or policy issue at either the national or local level. One of the best-known of these front organizations was the Committee Against Summit Entanglements, a group formed by Robert Welch to protest a proposed exchange of state visits by Eisenhower and Khrushchev in 1959.[7] A member of this group's executive committee was Barry Goldwater, and his association with this organization was given extended treatment by the press during his campaign in 1964. More recently, rightist organizations such as the John Birch Society were actively involved in George Wallace's bid for the presidency in 1968.

Many activities, policies, positions, and other details about contemporary rightist personalities and movements have been discussed in a large popular and scholarly literature that has grown steadily since the McCarthy era (1950–1954). It includes a number of articles in the national picture magazines that were intensely critical of the methods, persons, and goals of most of these formal organizations, particularly the John Birch Society.[8] As we shall see, the critical posture of the

[6]See Hanna Wartenburg and Wagner Thielens, "Against the United Nations: A Letter-Writing Campaign by the Birch Movement," mimeographed (New York: Bureau of Applied Social Research, Columbia University, 1964); and James McEvoy with Mark Chesler and Richard Schmuck, "Letters from the Right: Content Analysis of a Letter-Writing Campaign" (Ann Arbor: Institute for Social Research, University of Michigan, 1966).

[7]See Robert Welch, *The Blue Book of the John Birch Society* (Belmont, Mass.: John Birch Society, 1961), p. 117 (unnumbered), for reproduction of this committee's advertisements, which had appeared in ninety-seven newspapers at the time of the *Blue Book*'s publication.

[8]For further description of the scope and methods of the political actions of the *organizations* that compose the contemporary right, the following sources offer accounts that vary greatly in their distance from the subject: Ralph E. Ellsworth and Sarah M. Harris, *The American Right Wing: A Report to the Fund for the Republic* (Washington, D.C.: Public Affairs Press, 1962); Harry and Bonaro Overstreet, *The Strange Tactics of Extremism* (New York: Norton, 1964); Ross

press evidently had a substantial effect on the attitudes of the mass public; for as the population became informed of that organization's existence, it developed, by and large, rather hostile opinions of it.

VISIBILITY OR GROWTH? CHANGES IN PERCEPTIONS AND SUPPORT OF THE AMERICAN RIGHT

Despite the growth of the literature purporting to expose or document the behavior of contemporary rightist organizations, very little is known about the full extent of support for rightist groups or their policies among the mass public. At this point, then, let us consider two questions that are somewhat more directly related to our inquiry: Has there, in fact, been a recent growth in the membership of rightist organizations and in mass support for these groups? Or is there simply a small set of rightist elites and formal organizations that lack a substantial following in the mass public but whose size and influence have been greatly magnified as the result of their high visibility in the mass media and their exposure in two recent national elections?

These questions demand consideration for several reasons, the most important of which is the fact that the size of an organization, its public support, and its visibility in the media (for example, Hell's Angels) are quite often independent (or negatively correlated) variables. This is particularly important not only because of the right's persistently high

R. Rice, *Extremist Politics: An Arizona Recall Election,* Eagleton Institute Series, case 33 (New York: McGraw-Hill, 1964).

An intensely negative but largely factual description of several major rightist groups is found in Arnold Forster and Benjamin Epstein, *Danger on the Right* (New York: Random House, 1964); and an unfortunately biased and journalistic interview study, *The John Birch Society,* has been done by J. Allen Broyles (Boston: Beacon Press, 1964). A large amount of information of uneven quality about these groups is available in the publications of Group Research, Inc., available by subscription only from Washington, D.C.

The empirical studies completed of the membership of these groups will be discussed in detail in a later chapter, but Schmuck and Chesler, "On Super-Patriotism," and the article by Alan F. Westin in *The Radical Right,* ed. Daniel Bell (New York: Doubleday Anchor Books, 1964), are also of value here.

Important works on the McCarthy period are: Earl Latham, *The Communist Controversy in Washington* (Cambridge: Harvard University Press, 1966); Richard Rovere, *Senator Joe McCarthy* (Cleveland: Meridian Books, 1960), which assigns much more political power to McCarthy than he in fact possessed; and Samuel Stouffer, *Communism, Conformity, and Civil Liberties* (New York: Doubleday, 1955). Most recently, Michael P. Rogin's *The Intellectuals and McCarthy: The Radical Specter* (Cambridge: M.I.T. Press, 1967) examines and refutes the thesis advanced by Richard Hofstadter and others that McCarthy's support was drawn from populist remnants of the population.

level of media exposure, but also because of the exaggerated assumptions that have often been made about the support for Joseph McCarthy, an early spokesman for the "new American right."[9]

The information available about the public's attitudes and opinions toward Senator McCarthy indicates that the number of potential members of a McCarthy-led social movement did not bulk very large in the American population. Samuel Stouffer, for example, found that only 8 percent of his combined national cross-section samples designated McCarthy as the national leader whose opinions on "how to handle United States Communists [they] would especially respect." Only 5 percent of his sample of community leaders gave the same response.[10] Moreover, Lipset notes in his summary of relevant poll data:

His [McCarthy's] seeming popularity was the result of his riding the existing powerful anti-Communist bandwagon, whose popular influence he may have ultimately reduced rather than enhanced by alienating the militant anti-Communists who believed in due process. . . . This conclusion does not mean that McCarthyism did not exist as a political force. There was a significant minority of Americans who strongly identified [with McCarthy]. . . . But this group of "McCarthyites" was probably always a minority, much smaller than the "anti-McCarthyites." . . .[11]

As Stouffer demonstrated, they were indeed a minority. There was never a large-scale social movement operating to sustain and follow McCarthy, nor was his behavior in the Senate the result of his being the representative of a major rightist constituency whose policy preferences he was, like any faithful instructed delegate, merely carrying out. Despite this, many persons and many social scientists responded to McCarthyism as though it enjoyed as great a level of social support as

[9]A grossly exaggerated and empirically unwarranted report of support for McCarthy is to be found in Hans Toch, *The Social Psychology of Social Movements* (Indianapolis: Bobbs-Merrill, 1965). In this and other cases, Toch has failed to examine even the most elementary evidence to support his claims about contemporary rightist groups. He comments: "McCarthy initiated a campaign which permeated every segment of American Life. He not only personally destroyed individuals and organizations but inspired others to suspect, to investigate and to blacklist. . . . In addition, distrust, suspicion and panic permeated all social interactions, and few Americans ventured to openly question the premise of domestic Communist subversion" (p. 61). Prior to this book's publication, there were at least four published studies, including, of course, the most important one by Stouffer, which demonstrate without question that Toch's statements concerning universal suspicion and panic are simply false.

[10]Stouffer, *Communism*, p. 230.

[11]Seymour Martin Lipset, "Three Decades of the Radical Right," in *Radical Right*, ed. Bell, pp. 392–93.

Nazism in Germany two decades earlier—a response hardly warranted by the facts.[12]

More recently, the nomination of Barry Goldwater by the Republican party in 1964 elicited a great deal of interest in a "new" rightist movement. As we shall see, support for Goldwater was not very strong, even among Republicans, and his nomination was favored by less than 10 percent of the electorate. Despite this, the Goldwater organization was sufficiently powerful to capture the decision-making arm of the Republican party—an important, though electorally disastrous, victory. Finally, the campaign of George Wallace for a time seemed to indicate the existence of a large body of support for an extremist movement that posed a serious threat to the two-party system. Whether or not one considers either of these movements to be successes or failures, it is well worth the effort to attempt an answer to the questions with which we began this section. Specifically, is the right static or dynamic? Has its increasing visibility in elections and the media been paralleled by significant increases in support among the mass public?

To begin, perhaps a demonstration of the response of the mass media to several contemporary rightist formal organizations will be sufficient to show how confusion might arise between the increasing visibility of a group in the media and its actual public support.

Figure I.1 was constructed by measuring the number of column inches devoted to five contemporary rightist organizations in the *New York Times Index* from 1958 through 1967. Since the column width and type size remained constant during all these years, such a measurement, while by no means as accurate as an actual analysis of the articles themselves, provides a rough indication of the relative change in the visibility of these groups in an American newspaper distinguished for its lack of sensationalistic journalism. As a brief examination of this figure indicates, any consistent reader of the *Times* throughout this period would have been exposed to about twenty times as much in-

12For an extensive discussion of McCarthy's supposed power in and out of the Senate, see Nelson W. Polsby, "Toward an Explanation of McCarthyism," in *Politics and Social Life,* ed. Nelson W. Polsby, Robert A. Dentler, and Paul Smith (Boston: Houghton Mifflin, 1963), pp. 809–24. In his analyses of the case of Senator Benton of Connecticut and of the mass support for McCarthy, Polsby concludes that even with the evidence available during McCarthy's tenure in the Senate, it would have been possible to demonstrate with some conviction that his supposed power was not, in fact, very great. Polsby's arguments in this article, published in 1960, demonstrate both the inadequacies of data collection about McCarthy by the polling organizations and the failure of the theorists of the McCarthy phenomenon to take advantage of even the limited data available on the issue. See especially pp. 818–21.

FIGURE I.1

Sum of Column Inches in *New York Times Index*
Devoted to Five Conservative or Superpatriotic
Organizations,* 1958–1967

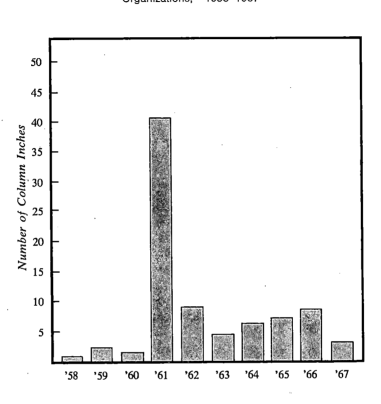

*The groups were, by year of appearance, Americans for Con-
stitutional Action (1958), Freedoms Foundation (1959), John Birch
Society (1961), Christian Anti-Communism Crusade (1961), and
Young Americans for Freedom (1961).

formation about rightist organizations after 1960 as he would have
been before that time. The dramatic increase in visibility of these five
groups in 1961 resulted in large part from the appearance of the John
Birch Society, whose existence had been exposed in that year, although
it was actually founded in 1958. In 1961 the *Times Index* contained
thirty-seven and one-half column inches of references to the society;
the following year it devoted three inches to it, but gave the Young

Americans for Freedom almost four and one-half inches of space. In 1965 the John Birch Society again received the bulk of all rightist references, with over five inches of space given over to it, and it continued to be the dominant, though declining, rightist organization through 1967.[13]

The contemporary right has also, of course, received immense amounts of publicity as a result of the controversy over the issue of extremism which split the Republican elites at the Republican national convention of 1964, and which was in part responsible for the defection of a number of traditionally Republican and independent voters in the election of that year. In 1964 "extremism" came to be synonymous with rightist organizations, especially the John Birch Society, and Goldwater's seeming defense of such organizations in his acceptance speech at the convention became a *cause célèbre* from the very beginning of his campaign. While Wallace's candidacy did not excite so much intra-party venom as the Goldwater campaign, it also drew considerable attention from columnists and pundits, many of whom saw it, quite correctly I believe, as a serious manifestation of rightist and populistic impulses over and above its overt racial basis.

A Gallup poll taken in February 1962 revealed that only 58 percent of the American population had even heard of the John Birch Society, despite the already large amounts of publicity it had then received. By the end of 1964, 79 percent of the electorate had heard of the society, an increase of 21 percent.[14] Has the growing visibility of rightist formal organizations, in particular the John Birch Society, and the growing knowledge about these organizations among the mass public been accompanied by an indication that these organizations are rapidly expanding their appeals to the American people? The available data on this question are, unfortunately, highly ambiguous, and it is difficult to determine exactly how much, if any, real growth in support of the John Birch Society has actually occurred from February 1962 through December 1964, the period when the society's name became generally known to the mass public.

Data from the 1962 Gallup survey and the 1964 postelection study of the Survey Research Center suggest at first glance that support for the John Birch Society may have increased between February 1962 and January 1965 by approximately 100 percent. If an expression of a

[13]*New York Times Index* (New York: Times Publishing Co., 1958–1965).

[14]Gallup poll, February 1962, reported in Lipset, "Three Decades" pp. 422–27; and the 1964 election study of the Survey Research Center University of Michigan.

favorable attitude toward the society is taken as a rough but reasonably meaningful indication of potential political support or possible affilia-tion, these and two other surveys provide some very limited information about the changes in support during the approximately three-year period between them and are, in any case, the best measures that are available for this time period.

Table I.2 shows the divisions of opinion regarding the John Birch Society disclosed by the Gallup poll of February 1962. Lipset, who completed an analysis of the data in this poll, found that Birch support

TABLE I.2

Support for John Birch Society,
February 1962

Opinion	*Percentage* (*N* = 1,616)
Favorable	5%
Unfavorable	26
No opinion	27
Don't know about society	42
Total	100%

was highest among college graduates and that, as would be expected, knowledge of the society's existence was disproportionately high among respondents in the upper income and better educated strata of the population. Since only 58 percent of the population at that time knew of the existence of the society, however, Lipset suggested that latent support for it might exist among that segment of the population which had not then heard of it, specifically the less educated and lower income groups in the population.

As I noted, by January 1965 79 percent of the American popula-tion of voting age claimed to have heard of the John Birch Society. This figure appears to be very close to the saturation point of knowledge of contemporary political organizations among the American public. For example, the American Communist party is known to 80 percent of the population, the NAACP to 82 percent, CORE to 70 percent, the Black Muslims to 75 percent, and the Ku Klux Klan to 90 percent.[15]

What changes has this increased diffusion of knowledge about the John Birch Society introduced into the patterns and level of support for this organization? First, consider the responses to an item in the 1964

[15]Based on responses to questions concerning these groups in the 1964 post-election study of the Survey Research Center. This is probably an overstatement of the real level of knowledge.

TABLE I.3

Distribution of Feelings Toward John Birch Society of Respondents Knowing of Its Existence, November 1964–January 1965

0°–9°	10°–19°	20°–29°	30°–39°	40°–49°	50°–59°	60°–69°	70°–79°	80°–89°	90°–100°
30.4%	7.6%	2.2%	7.7%	4.7%	36.0%	4.4%	4.0%	2.1%	.9%

TABLE I.4

Data from Table I.3 Grouped by 0°–49°, 50°–59°, and 60°–100°

0°–49°	50°–59°	60°–100°
52.6%	36.0%	11.4%

Survey Research Center's postelection study asking respondents who had an opinion of the John Birch Society to indicate their feelings toward it by locating it on a "feeling thermometer," a card that has a scale from 0 degrees (least favorable feeling) to 100 degrees (most favorable), with a 50-degree neutral point. Tables I.3 and I.4 report the responses to this item.

The meaning of these data is uncertain. On the one hand, if any response greater than 59 degrees is considered the equivalent of a response of "favorable" to the Gallup survey's question on opinions of the society, support for this organization has increased by more than 120 percent since February 1962. Nevertheless, as an inspection of Table I.3 indicates, the level of approval at the extremely favorable end of the feeling thermometer is very low, with only 3 percent of the respondents giving a response of 80 degrees or more. A similar but less difficult problem occurs with the unfavorable responses, which appear, when grouped in Table I.4, to have also increased by more than 100 percent since the Gallup survey. In this case, however, the great majority (38 percent out of 53 percent) of responses below 50 degrees fall in the 0–19-degree range, suggesting clear-cut disapproval of the organization on the part of many respondents.

Since we know that the majority of changes in levels of approval are to be found in the lower income and education levels of the population, it is tempting to infer that true support has increased among those groups, as indicated by the 11.4 percent of the responses falling above 59 degrees. Unfortunately, no such inference is justified because of the fact that persons from these socioeconomic strata do not tend to give reliable responses to items on the feeling thermometer. (Nor would they be likely to do so with favorable/unfavorable dichotomies, either.)[16] For example, the correlation between responses to the categories "liberals" and "conservatives" on the thermometer is *positive* among these respondents; only among persons of higher levels of education, income, and information do these scales produce the expected negative correlation.[17] If, however, we examine these scores by level of education

[16]The problem raised here, attitudinal consistency and the validity of the measures of approval and support, has not been pursued further because of the very small *N*s involved in the approving subsets of the sample. A brief discussion of the validity of the Birch support measure, however, appears in chap. 3.

[17]For respondents with an eighth-grade education or less, the correlations between liberals and conservatives were Gamma = +.162, Tau Beta = +.199. For respondents with a college education or more, the correlations were Gamma = −.442, Tau Beta = −.384. These data were supplied through the courtesy of Mr. Richard Katz of the Inter-University Consortium for Political Research of the Institute for Social Research, University of Michigan.

attained by the respondents (Table I.5), we find that there is an increase in approval of the John Birch Society of more than 10 percentage points since 1962, when only 8 percent of the respondents in the Gallup poll with comparable education responded with approval to the interviewer's question about the organization.[18] Perhaps this means that support for the society has increased; but it may simply indicate that the dichotomous (favorable/unfavorable) phrasing of the Gallup item forced college-educated respondents to choose between qualified or unqualified approval of the organization, and that qualified approval was registered as disapproval.

TABLE I.5

Support for John Birch Society by Level of Education
with Grouped Responses on Feeling Thermometer

Feeling-Thermometer Score	*Educational Attainment*							
	Grade School		*High School*		*Some College*		*College Graduate*	
	N	*%*	*N*	*%*	*N*	*%*	*N*	*%*
<49°	184	26.7%	196	40.0%	99	50.0%	116	66.7%
50°–59°	193	28.0	149	30.3	43	21.7	26	14.9
>60°	313	45.3	146	29.7	56	28.3	32	18.4
Total	690	100.0%	491	100.0%	198	100.0%	174	100.0%

This problem is all the more difficult to resolve because of the fact that another Gallup survey in August 1964 revealed that there had been no change in the level of support for the John Birch Society during the twenty-nine months since the February 1962 poll—at least as measured by the favorable/unfavorable item. By August 1964, however, 67 percent of the population had an opinion of the society, and the level of disapproval had increased from 43 percent to 59 percent. This poll indicates that many of the less informed persons in the population who had not heard of the society in February of 1962 decided, upon hearing about it, that they opposed it. Thus if any increase in support for the society has occurred, it has probably been within the segment of the population (12 percent) that became aware of its existence sometime between August 1964 and January 1965, the date of completion of the Survey Research Center survey. Given the problems of comparative analysis of the Gallup and SRC surveys on this issue, it is

[18]Lipset, "Three Decades," pp. 422–27.

impossible to make any definite statement about the growth or decline of support for the John Birch Society in the period between February 1962 and January 1965 using the survey data discussed here. However, there is no clear evidence that any substantial gain in support actually occurred.

In December of 1965, however, Gallup again polled a national sample about their attitudes toward the John Birch Society, but did not employ the dichotomous favorable/unfavorable item. Instead, the Gallup interviewers asked their respondents to locate the society on a scale very similar in construction to the Survey Research Center's feeling thermometer. The Gallup scale has a range of possible responses, from +5 (the most favorable) to −5 (the most negative). There is no neutral point. While the Gallup release on this poll does not indicate the percentage of responses to each interval of the scale, Gallup reports that 3 percent of his sample responded with a +5, the most favorable ranking possible. If the Gallup and SRC scales are comparable in that they elicit more accurately differentiated opinions and that a +5 on the Gallup scale is the equivalent of a ranking of 90 degrees or more on the SRC feeling thermometer, then it appears that, even with the relatively high percentage of the population that knew of the existence of the John Birch Society, there was no significant increase in support for it in the period from January to December of 1965, even though persons who first heard of the society during this period probably formed the last reservoir of potential support for the organization. The SRC study found 0.9 percent of their sample above 90 degrees, thus differing from the Gallup survey by little more than 2 percentage points. There is no reason to assume that the two scales are perfectly comparable, however, and Gallup reports that his December 1965 poll elicited a 33 percent "no opinion" response, which is, of course, much higher than was found in the SRC sample (taken eleven months prior to the Gallup sample), in which 79 percent of the respondents offered an opinion of the society.

Thus, despite the existence of four national surveys spanning a period of almost four years, during which the John Birch Society became a national political issue and a large majority of the population developed attitudes toward it, it is impossible to say with conviction what the real level of support for the society was at any time during this period or what changes occurred in the level of support as public knowledge of the society increased. It is clear, however, that the vast majority of the American population now has very unfavorable attitudes toward the society, and it also appears that there probably has not been any large increase in the level of its support since the first national survey was taken in February of 1962.[19] Questions concerning the John Birch Society were dropped from the 1968 SRC studies, making its status indeterminate as far as mass support or opposition is concerned.

Aside from these data about the level of support for the John Birch Society in the mass public, is there evidence to suggest that the increasing visibility of the organized right in the mass media is based upon the fact that there has been a growing commitment to rightist political organizations and political activities by that segment of the population *already* predisposed to support rightist causes and formal organizations? That is, are those persons who formerly had a more passive orientation toward the implementation of their rightist political beliefs now becoming sufficiently mobilized so that they might be termed an interest group, whereas before, in Dahrendorf's terms, they would have composed merely a quasi group?[20] If, on the basis of the polls cited above, we assume that, at a minimum, 5 percent of Americans over twenty-one years of age express moderate or strong support for the John Birch Society, and if we also assume that other rightist organizations would also be supported by persons favoring the society, then there are approximately 5.4 million persons in the United States who form such a quasi group.[21] What evidence is there to indicate that, among these persons, there has been an increase in the level of political activity of a rightist nature?

Again, as was the case with the poll data, the available information bearing on this question is limited in both quantity and quality. But in the face of the fact that the American right has had such large amounts of media visibility and also because it seems to have had considerable success in influencing the decisions of the Republican party, it seems important to attempt an answer to this question, if only because of the implications that such an answer might have for the study of political pressure groups. Accordingly, one measure of increasing mobilization of this segment of the population—periodical circulation—will be explored in some detail in an effort to decide if the American right is simply an elitist phenomenon or if in fact it enjoys any significant support in the segment of the population that appears to offer potential support for formal rightist organizations.

[19]The data from the August 1964 and December 1965 Gallup polls were supplied by the American Institute of Public Opinion (the Gallup organization) and are from news releases of August 5, 1964, and December 19, 1965.

[20]Ralf Dahrendorf, *Class and Class Conflict in Industrial Society* (Stanford, Calif.: Stanford University Press, 1959), pp. 157–205.

[21]U.S. Department of Commerce, Bureau of the Census, *Statistical Abstract of the United States, 1966* (Washington D.C.: U.S. Government Printing Office, 1966), p. 23.

17

I selected periodical circulation as an index because for the most part it is an uncontaminated indication of self-initiated interest in the ideas expressed in the periodicals. Unlike financial contributions, the circulation of periodicals is not subject to violent inflation by the actions of a few individuals, although artificially high levels of circulation can sometimes be maintained by free distribution of periodicals as the result of subsidy. Secondly, accurate time-series statistics are available for both rightist and nonrightist publications, providing some normative data about the behavior of rightist periodicals; finally there are, to my knowledge, no accurate or even fairly reliable reports of membership figures or growth rates made by any of the major American rightist organizations, and estimates compiled by groups such as the Committee on Political Education (COPE) of the AFL-CIO are, in my judgment, unreliable.

In 1960, thirteen rightist periodicals had an average circulation total of 417,961 copies per issue. By 1965, twenty (including the original thirteen) rightist publications had nearly doubled this figure, with a total circulation of 727,256 copies per issue. The most striking gains during this period were made by a set of rightist periodicals that were recommended by the John Birch Society to its members. In 1960 there were seven recommended periodicals with a total circulation of 101,261 per issue; by 1965 there were ten Birch-recommended publications with a circulation of 332,886, an increase of 228 percent. The most widely circulated publication during this period was *Human Events,* a conservative weekly newspaper published in Washington, D.C., which reprints a number of editorials and news stories from major American newspapers as well as featuring conservative and rightist columnists and sponsoring political action campaigns of a conservative nature. In the years 1960–1965, *Human Events* grew by more than 280 percent; from the first year for which reliable circulation figures are available (1953) to the present time, its circulation has increased more than 900 percent. Less impressive increases, and some decreases, in circulation occurred among rightist periodicals that did not receive the recommendation of the John Birch Society. Circulation figures that are available for unrecommended periodicals show that in 1960 these publications had a total circulation of 316,700 per issue; by 1965 this figure had advanced only 24 percent, to 394,370.

What, if anything, may be learned from these data? Before attempting to draw inferences from them, we must raise three questions bearing on their interpretation: First, do these data retain any importance if they are compared with growth rates of other periodicals in the period 1960–1965? Secondly, does the fact that a number of the rightist periodicals in this group are new suggest that their growth curves are necessarily parabolic, and that they therefore evidence no greater rates of increase than do other periodicals in their initial stages of circulation growth? Finally, does the differential rate of increase between periodicals recommended by the John Birch Society and other rightist periodicals reflect the influence of the society or something in the unrecommended media which might have caused them to decline even if they had received the society's recommendation?

FIGURE I.2

Percentage Increase in Average Circulation per Issue
of Rightist, Liberal and Leftist, "Intellectual," and
Popular Periodicals, 1960–1965

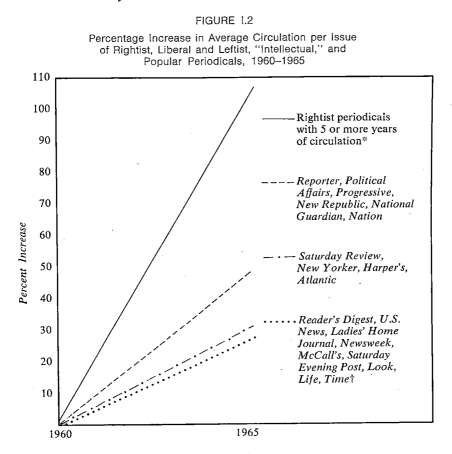

Christian Beacon, Dan Smoot Report, Human Events, National Review, The Wanderer, Weekly Crusader, Christian Crusade, The Citizen, The Cross and the Flag, Free Enterprise, Common Sense, Modern Age.

†There were no important differences between the news magazines and the other popular magazines, so they are combined in this figure. The news magazines' growth rate was 25.3 percent, compared with the other popular magazines' rate of 25.6 percent in the period cited.

Figure I.2 indicates the mean percentage of increase of four types of periodicals from 1960 through 1965. Rightist periodicals include only those publications that have a history of five or more years of publication. The other three groups of publications were selected to represent leftist or liberal political magazines, serious, somewhat intellectually oriented magazines, and magazines designed for mass consumption. It is clear from an inspection of this figure that rightist publications enjoyed a substantially higher rate of growth than other periodicals during the same five-year period. Thus, even though it is uncertain whether this high growth rate actually reflects a growing mobilization of potential rightists or simply follows the early growth patterns of any set of new publications, it is obvious that rightist periodicals, like rightist voluntary associations, became conspicuously visible from 1960 through 1965.

The most serious problem of interpretation of these data is implied in the paragraph above—namely, what is the normal early growth pattern for a new publication? Since the most remarkable rates of growth have been found in rightist publications that are relatively new compared with the other publications in Figure I.2 and which have received the recommendation of the John Birch Society, it is important to ask if these increases are due to the recency of the magazines' founding, or are larger than would be expected for newly established magazines. Figure I.3, while based on an extremely small sample of the four types of magazines represented in Figure I.2, indicates that magazines, especially ones of general interest, do indeed have a very rapid rate of growth during the first fifteen years of their publication. However, several serious questions about the meaning of this figure (aside from the size of the sample of publications used in its construction) make it very doubtful if it is at all appropriate to make comparisons between such magazines as *Life* and either the *New Leader* or the *Dan Smoot Report*. This is because the growth curves of mass-circulation magazines such as *Life* and *Look* are in large part a function of high advertising revenues, which permit such publications to price their products below the cost of production. The economics of this strategy are described by Theodore Peterson in his *Magazines in the Twentieth Century* as a basic principle of the mass marketing of magazines: ". . . A publisher could lose millions of dollars on circulation by selling his magazine at less than production cost and yet could reap millions of dollars in profit from advertising. . . ."[22] None of the political magazines in Figures I.2 and I.3, with the possible exception

[22]Theodore B. Peterson, *Magazines in the Twentieth Century* (Urbana: University of Illinois Press, 1964), p. 25.

FIGURE I.3

Initial Growth Rates of Four Groups of American Periodicals at
Five- and Fifteen-Year Intervals After Date of Founding

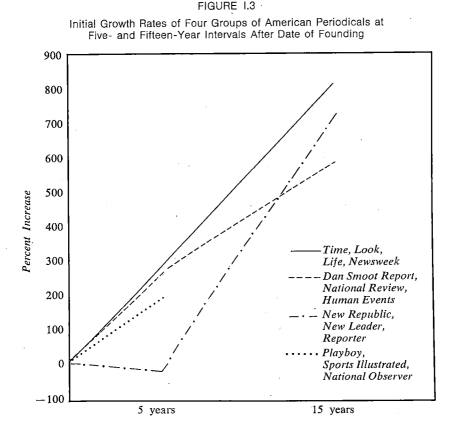

of *The Reporter* (no longer published), has anything like a subsidy provided by high advertising incomes. Some of the rightist and leftist periodicals, such as the *New Republic* and the *National Review,* do have limited privately funded subsidies, but they are not sufficiently large to permit unlimited deficit financing of a high level of circulation.[23] Therefore, publishers of most political magazines must look to subscription and newsstand sales of their publications as well as advertising for whatever income they earn from their products. They cannot

[23]The *National Review* has operated at a deficit of about $100,000 per year since it was founded by William F. Buckley. This deficit has been repaid to the publisher by subscribers who have each year responded to an appeal for funds to liquidate the past year's operating losses. In 1967 the *National Review* was involved in an expensive lawsuit with Dr. Linus Pauling, which increased the *Review*'s operating deficit to $250,000.

21

expand their circulation through the use of artificially low prices, as do the mass-circulation magazines, even if a market for political magazines existed that could be exploited by such methods. Figure I.3, therefore, must be read in a somewhat different light. The fact that the growth rates of the three long-term Birch-recommended publications have almost kept pace with the growth curves of the mass-circulation magazines founded in the 1920s and 1930s, and that they have exceeded the growth curve of three of the newest and most successful general publications, *Playboy, Sports Illustrated,* and the *National Observer,* gives some limited support to the proposition that there has been a disproportionately high rate of growth among rightist periodicals.

Finally, unlike the three liberal or leftist political magazines for which initial circulation figures are available, the rightist periodicals have shown a consistent pattern of growth from their beginnings. The liberal periodicals in Figure I.3 have also had a high rate of growth— but the figure is particularly high because one of them, *The Reporter,* grew by more than 2,000 percent between 1954 and 1964. Figure I.4 shows that the combined rate of growth for all newer and older rightist publications was slightly higher than the combined growth rate of newer and older magazines designed for mass consumption and of liberal and leftist periodicals.

The meaning of Figure I.4 is limited because the sample of periodicals is very small and also because it was necessarily constructed from available data, thus excluding all publications without either published circulation reports in Ayer's *Guide* or second-class mailing permits. Even given these limitations, however, two possible interpretations of these data may be advanced. First, since it is certain that the absolute level of increase in circulation among rightist periodicals since 1960 has been very large, it is very likely that an increasing number of persons are interesting themselves in rightist ideas and ideology. If this is not the case, and the growth in circulation of these periodicals reflects an increasing consumption of rightist publications by a relatively fixed number of rightists in the population, it is evident that this set of individuals is becoming extraordinarily involved with rightist media.

The last question to be discussed is the possible cause of the differential rates of growth between the periodicals recommended by the John Birch Society and those other rightist publications for which circulation figures are available and which did not receive the society's recommendation.

As I noted earlier, the recommended publications grew by 228 percent between 1960 and 1965, and in the same period the non-recommended magazines grew by 24 percent, a rate just slightly below

FIGURE I.4

Combined Growth Rates of New and Old Periodicals with
Five or More Years of Publication, 1960–1965

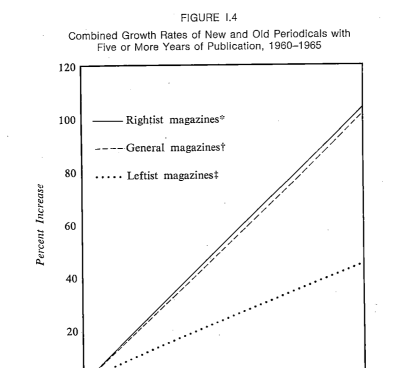

*Human Events, National Review, Dan Smoot Report, Christian
Beacon, The Wanderer, Weekly Crusader, Christian Crusade, The
Citizen, The Cross and the Flag, Free Enterprise, Common Sense,
Modern Age.*
†*Life, Look, McCall's, Ladies' Home Journal, Reader's Digest, Satur-
day Evening Post, Atlantic, Harper's, Saturday Review of Literature,
New Yorker, Time, Newsweek, U.S. News and World Report, National
Observer, Sports Illustrated, Playboy.*
‡*Reporter, New Republic, Progressive, Nation, National Guardian,
Political Affairs.*

that of the normal (25 percent) growth rate of the national mass-
circulation news and general-interest magazines cited in Figure I.4.

While the endorsement of the John Birch Society probably had
something to do with the circulation increases of the recommended
periodicals, it seems equally likely that such increases have been the
result of the fact that most of these periodicals have confined themselves largely to political matters, and have avoided many of the themes
so often found in some of the older rightist publications, such as anti-

Semitism, religious fundamentalism, and overt racism. *Common Sense,* for example, a magazine noted for its hostility to Jews, declined in circulation from 84,000 in 1960 to 52,000 in 1965. At the same time, however, the circulation of *The Cross and the Flag,* also anti-Jewish, increased, but not enough to make up for the decrease in the circulation of *Common Sense.* Between 1946 and 1959 there was a corresponding decline of overt anti-Semitism in the United States. In 1946, 64 percent of the population reported hearing "criticism" against the Jews; by 1959 this had declined to 12 percent.[24]

This explanation is by no means certain and it is offered simply as a suggestion. Since no data whatsoever exist to explain this difference other than the initial growth-rate curves, the question remains unanswered. Nevertheless, it is clear that the most widely circulated and fastest growing periodicals of the American right are presenting a modernistic approach to their readers in the sense that they are discussing political affairs from ideological positions that have, by and large, excluded overt racism, anti-Semitism, and religious fundamentalism from their foundations.

CONCLUSION

Although four national surveys have dealt with the question of support and potential growth of the John Birch Society, no clear answer has emerged. There are indications that there is no large body of support for the John Birch Society, and that there has been no important increase in support for it as knowledge of the society's existence has been disseminated through the American mass public. It is clear, in any case, that the great majority of the population holds negative views of this organization. On the other hand, although the relevant evidence is admittedly very limited, in my opinion an analysis of the circulation figures of rightist and other periodicals supports the hypothesis that there has been a disproportionate increase in interest in rightist media within the small segment of the American population willing to support the organized right.

[24]Bruno Bettelheim and Morris Janowitz, *Social Change and Prejudice* (New York: Free Press, Macmillan, 1964), p. 8.

CHAPTER II

Social and Psychological
Origins of the Right:
Some Theoretical Considerations

PARALLELING THE RISE of the modern totalitarian state has been an effort by social scientists to identify the factors in both personalities and societies which have made possible the initial successes and relative permanence of absolutist governments in twentieth-century industrial states. In addition to many excellent historical treatments of Naziism, fascism, Stalinist communism, and the like, there are two broad research traditions that have attempted to discover the origins of totalitarianism through an examination of both social and psychological variables. The most highly formalized of these traditions, developed within psychology, is concerned with the authoritarian personality, a psychological type that is presumably predisposed to successful integration in a totalitarian social order.

The second tradition arose from the disciplines of history, political science, and sociology, and, although there are a number of discrete subfields within this tradition, it may be roughly described by the term "mass society": a society characterized by high levels of industrialization, the availability of large numbers of nonelites for political mobilization, and the ready accessibility of elites for influence and replacement. Many authors see alienation and political isolation accompanying the development of mass society. This results from the formation of a rootless, anomic "mass man," and is manifested in political irresponsibility and easy mobilization by unscrupulous elites. Others, however, point out that the increasing bureaucratization and extensive differentiation of occupational roles in some societies are accompanied by potentials for increased individual freedom provided by national economic planning and the rise of the welfare ethic.[1] Many theorists of mass society may be described as pluralists. Their vision of a stable, libertarian society rests on the concept of a diffusion of power among competing groups. Society, they believe, is rendered more stable by the cross-cutting allegiances and responsiveness to political demands which they assume accompany a pluralist order.

The scholarly literature of these two fields is immense. A recent review[2] of social-psychological research on authoritarianism lists over 250 published studies that have employed the concepts and scales developed originally by T. W. Adorno, Else Frenkel-Brunswik, Daniel J. Levinson, and R. Nevitt Sanford in *The Authoritarian Personality.*[3] Some of this literature has been severely critical[4] of the methodological procedures used by these authors and of their supposedly liberal biases; but despite these criticisms, authoritarianism has become an important and lasting area of concern in social science, and as a result it has been both directly and indirectly influential in several of the theories that have been developed to account for the contemporary American right.[5] Presumably the use of this concept in the formulation of some of the theories about rightists is the result of the obvious similarities between the ideology of the American right and the descriptions of authoritarianism provided by Adorno *et al.* Authoritarianism by itself,

[1] Edward Shils, "The Theory of Mass Society," in *America as a Mass Society,* ed. Philip Olson (New York: Free Press, Macmillan, 1963), pp. 30–47.

[2] John P. Kirscht and Ronald C. Dillehay, "Social Psychological Research on Authoritarianism: A Review," mimeographed (Ann Arbor: School of Public Health, University of Michigan, 1966).

[3] T. W. Adorno, Else Frenkel-Brunswik, Daniel J. Levinson, and R. Nevitt Sanford, *The Authoritarian Personality* (New York: Harper, 1950).

[4] See especially R. Christie and Marie Jahoda, eds., *Studies in the Scope and Method of the Authoritarian Personality* (Glencoe, Ill.: Free Press, 1954).

[5] A brilliant review of the debate on this issue occurs in Roger Brown, *Social Psychology* (New York: Free Press, Macmillan, 1965), pp. 447–546. Brown concludes his discussion as follows:

"My conclusion, then, is that it has not been demonstrated that fascists and communists resemble one another in authoritarianism or in any other dimension of ideology. No one thus far has shown that there is an authoritarian of the left. Still the impression persists that such a type exists and that some communists belong to it. I believe that Rokeach and the Berkeley authors [Adorno *et al.*] have, at several points in their writings, hit upon a promising characterization of general authoritarianism but it is not the characterization they develop or use as the basis of their scales. Perhaps the authoritarian is a person who is best characterized by the kind of information that will induce him to change his attitudes. ... The authoritarian will reverse his evaluations on the simple say-so of an authority figure ... [p. 542]."

however, has seldom been used as the single explanatory variable in studies of McCarthyism or of the contemporary right.[6] More often it has been linked with studies of tolerance, both ethnic and political, and it is around the question of political tolerance that it has had its greatest influence in the construction of theories about the origins of the American right.[7]

The mass-society research tradition has an even larger theoretical literature associated with it. The writers in this tradition include many prominent political and social theorists of the twentieth century, including José Ortega y Gasset, Joseph A. Schumpeter, David Riesman, Hannah Arendt, Erich Fromm, Edward Shils, Harold O. Laswell, and William Kornhauser. Unlike the literature on authoritarianism, however, the mass-society literature makes little use of empirical and non-experimental research. Indeed, empirical evaluation of many of the propositions of mass-society theory would be difficult if not impossible.

Since much of mass-society theory stems directly from a concern with German and Italian fascism and its origins in prewar European society, many of its premises appear to rest on the economic and political dislocations that affected almost every discernible social group in the European fascist nations from 1920 to 1933.[8] Although a succinct statement of the relationships among mass society, institutional weakness, "mass man," and support for extremist political movements is very difficult to find, the following passage from William Kornhauser's *The Politics of Mass Society* provides a general idea of the connections among them:

Mass movements depend for their success on the weakness of existing institutions and on the intensive support of large numbers of people. The

[6]The major exception is again found in Hans Toch, *The Social Psychology of Social Movements* (Indianapolis: Bobbs-Merrill, 1965), pp. 60–70. See chap. 1, n. 10.

[7]Martin Trow, "Right-Wing Radicalism and Political Intolerance: A Study of Support for McCarthy in a New England Town" (unpublished Ph.D. dissertation, Columbia University, 1957). See the discussion of the application of authoritarianism to the study of totalitarianism by Else Frenkel-Brunswik, "Environmental Controls and the Impoverishment of Thought," in *Totalitarianism*, ed. Carl J. Friedrich (Cambridge: Harvard University Press, 1954), pp. 171–202. This essay gives considerable attention to the integration of authoritarianism as a psychological state and social-structural conditions acting to encourage or extinguish its presence in a population. See also Herbert McClosky, "Conservatism and Personality," *American Political Science Review*, 52 (March 1958): 27–45. McClosky finds that conservatives share many of the supposed characteristics of authoritarians, such as intolerance and generalized hostility.

[8]An excellent account of the social-structural conditions surrounding the Nazi movement's rise to power is found in Hadley Cantril, *The Psychology of Social Movements* (New York: Science Editions, 1963), pp. 223–29.

weakness of organizations in mass society allows them to be penetrated by mass movements. The population then becomes more easily absorbed by means of these captured organizations (as well as by direct mobilization in a movement), including satellite organizations designed to reach unorganized masses. . . . Totalitarian movements in particular mobilize people who are "available" by virtue of being socially alienated.[9]

It has often been assumed that these socially alienated persons, presumably characterized by a disruption in their interpersonal relations and their roles in the division of labor, found their way into groups supporting Senator Joseph McCarthy and more recently into the John Birch Society and other contemporary rightist organizations. Moreover, alienation has frequently been employed as an explanatory variable in a set of propositions about the origins of the American right known as "status discrepancy" theories. This set of ideas, while exceedingly diffuse, has had a strong influence on some of the empirical research that has been conducted on the American right since 1955, when *The New American Right*,[10] in which these ideas were collected and related to traditional mass-society theory, was published.

Stated in their simplest form, these theories employ the dual concepts of class politics and status politics. Class politics, occurring during periods of economic dislocation, is characterized by economic class alignments that result in the breakdown of the usual cross-cutting political loyalties of a population and produce movements that concentrate on reallocation of economic resources in the society. Status politics gives rise to extremist political movements in societies not disorganized by economic depression, but where economic expansion produces structural strains among the various strata of the system. These strains sometimes take the form of incongruent status locations among segments of a population, and the results of their presence in a system are presumably similar to the alienation and anomie attributed to the development of mass society. An example of the continuing presence of this general set of ideas in recent research on the American right is found in Lipset's contribution to *The Radical Right*,[11] the second and revised edition of *The New American Right*. Lipset begins his discussion of the nature of extremist groups with the following extended citation from Edward Shils's *The Torment of Secrecy:*

[9]William Kornhauser, *The Politics of Mass Society* (Glencoe, Ill.: Free Press, 1959), p. 177.

[10]Daniel Bell, ed., *The New American Right* (New York: Criterion Books, 1955).

[11]Seymour Martin Lipset, "Three Decades of the Radical Right," in *The Radical Right*, ed. Daniel Bell (New York: Doubleday Anchor Books, 1964).

An extremist group is an alienated group. . . . It cannot share that sense of affinity to persons, of attachment to the institutions which confine political conflicts to peaceful solutions. . . . The romantic reactionaries, aristocratic and populistic . . . allege that they wish to conserve tradition. In practice they regard tradition as dead or corrupt or pernicious and they think that they must wipe out all that exists in order to re-create the right kind of tradition. Neither . . . the Christian Front [of Father Coughlin] nor the most zealous populist followers of Senator McCarthy at his height found the living traditions of the society in which they lived worthy of conservation. They were convinced that they had fallen into the hands of corrupt politicians and had themselves become corrupt. . . .

The ideological extremists [of the left and right]—all extremists are inevitably ideological—because of their isolation from the world, feel menaced by unknown dangers. The paranoiac tendencies which are closely associated with their apocalyptic and aggressive outlook make them think that the ordinary world, from which their devotion to the ideal cuts them off, is not normal at all; they think it is a realm of secret machinations. What goes on in the world of pluralistic politics, in civil society, is a secret to them. It is a secret which they must unmask by vigorous publicity. Their image of the "world" as the realm of evil, against which they must defend themselves and which they must ultimately conquer, forces them to think of their enemy's knowledge.[12]

As this analysis progresses I shall attempt to isolate what, precisely, it might be that makes people reject these traditions, if in fact they do. At the same time, of course, it may develop that the specific meaning of alienation for the groups covered by this analysis differs somewhat from Shils's diagnosis of their behavior, since he is presumably describing active affiliates of extremist organizations. Indeed, "alienation" may prove to be a very ambiguous description of their behavior. Now, however, let us look more closely at the theoretical and empirical literature that is most directly relevant to the questions raised in this volume, bearing in mind the general relationships that these theories have to the two traditions of mass society and authoritarianism.

The first major effort to account for the sociological origins of whatever segment it was of the American population that supported Senator McCarthy occurs in *The New American Right*. While there is an unfortunate absence of empirical data in this book, it is nevertheless full of novel ideas concerning the possible origins of McCarthy's supporters. The most important essays in the book from a sociological point of view (by Daniel Bell, Richard Hofstadter, and Seymour Martin

[12]Edward A. Shils, *The Torment of Secrecy: The Background and Consequences of American Security Policies* (Glencoe, Ill.: Free Press, 1956), pp. 231–34. Copyright © 1956 by The Free Press of Glencoe.

Lipset) concentrate on status anxiety. These ideas (while in part developed by Max Weber) grew out of Hofstadter's conception of a shift in America from class to status politics. Status groups were seen to have replaced classes as the primary agents of political protest. McCarthyism was seen by these authors as a protest against the "Eastern–Intellectual–State Department Establishment," which, so some authors thought, were perceived by the newly formed status protest groups, who supposedly supported McCarthy, as the prime symbolic obstacle in their course toward social advancement.

McCarthyism has often been equated with agrarian radicalism, particularly populism. This argument, as well as some of the pluralists' and ex-radicals' view of social movements generally, has been thoroughly questioned and soundly criticized in the recent and excellent volume by Michael Rogin, *The Intellectuals and McCarthy: The Radical Specter.*[13] Rogin's empirical analysis of this thesis is exhaustive, and I urge my readers to consult it directly for further discussion of the populist-agrarian question.

Nelson Polsby has compiled an amusing list of the social groups that were supposed to have supported McCarthy, according to some of the authors of *The New American Right*. Six out of seven of the essays in this volume named the new rich as supporters of McCarthy; five essays named Texans, Irish, and Germans; four named the middle class in general, Catholics, and midwesterners; three named the lower middle class, the upwardly mobile, and the less educated; and two named "cankered intellectuals," the old-family Protestant "shabby genteel," recent immigrants, the downwardly mobile, members of minority ethnic groups, old-guard Republicans, converted communists, and midwestern isolationists. The lower class, small-town lawyers, automobile dealers, oil wildcatters, real estate manipulators, proprietors of small businesses, manual workers, the elderly and retired, young people, the rentier class, southern Californians, South Bostonians, fringe urbanites in medium-sized cities, new arrivals in cities, Polish Catholics, "hick Protestants," members of patriotic and historical groups such as the D.A.R., Scandinavians, southern Protestant fundamentalists, soured patricians, small-town people, and neo-fascists were named in one essay each.[14] Clearly the supposed sources of McCarthy's support as suggested by the authors of *The New American Right* were nothing if not

[13]Michael P. Rogin, *The Intellectuals and McCarthy: The Radical Specter* (Boston: M.I.T. Press, 1967).

[14]Nelson W. Polsby, "Toward an Explanation of McCarthyism," in *Politics and Social Life*, ed. Nelson W. Polsby, Robert A. Dentler, and Paul Smith (Boston: Houghton Mifflin, 1963).

diffuse, and it is little to be wondered that the essays in this pioneer volume have generated considerable uncertainty about the origins of the right in the United States.

Other contributors to *The New American Right* saw McCarthyism as the result of increased international involvement on the part of the United States, which resulted in "important internal changes which have themselves been sources of strain, with the effect of superimposing one kind of strain on another."[15] Others, including Riesman, Glazer, Hofstadter, and Bell, advanced, in addition to the ideas of status politics, the notion that authoritarianism was at least in part responsible for McCarthy's support. Hofstadter, for example, sees authoritarianism linked with the child-rearing practices of status-striving adults: a child brought up in a status-striving home would be at once extraordinarily hostile and overly submissive to authority figures. Accordingly, given a potentially legitimate means to express hostility to authority, these authoritarians would have gratified their needs to defy authority by supporting McCarthy because of his attacks on and defiance of two major symbols of authority: the military and the government.[16] The tests required to establish the validity of such a theory are, unfortunately, beyond the scope of this book, or perhaps of any book.

Despite the ambiguities of the initial theories of the American right since 1955, a number of authors have refined and added empirical and empirically based theoretical knowledge about the right to the original set of hypotheses presented by the authors of *The New American Right*. Although some of this additional knowledge is restricted to a consideration of McCarthy's supporters alone, other works are based on an examination of partisans of newer rightist groups, such as the John Birch Society and the Christian Anti-Communism Crusade, which have been formed since 1955. Since there is, however, no great disjunction between these groups, at least insofar as theory construction is concerned, the additional studies reviewed below are at least of potentially equal relevance to an explanation of the contemporary right.

One of the first major papers to review the implications of the hypotheses in *The New American Right*, and one of the most important, was written by Nelson Polsby in 1960, while he was a graduate student at Yale.[17] Polsby's central concern was to evaluate the real versus the apparent political power of McCarthy, and much of his paper is concerned with the largely exaggerated power attributed to McCarthy by journalists, legislators, and a few social scientists. Arguing for a "policy

[15]Talcott Parsons, "Social Strains in America," in *Radical Right,* ed. Bell, p. 217.
[16]Richard Hofstadter, "The Pseudo-Conservative Revolt," in *ibid.,* pp. 89–90.
[17]Polsby, "Toward an Explanation of McCarthyism."

science" in which rational assessments of current political phenomena could and should be made by social scientists, Polsby shows that if politicians and government officials who opposed McCarthy had availed themselves of even the limited evidence available at that time, they would have established that the "power" McCarthy held over elected officials was, in fact, largely a myth.

Aside from this concern, however, Polsby also presents some limited tests of the three central explanatory hypotheses elaborated in *The New American Right:* authoritarianism, foreign involvement and its associated exogenous value strains, and status politics. He also re-tabulated several Gallup, Bean, and Harris surveys in an effort to identify the actual composition of the groups making up the American right (i.e., those groups supporting McCarthy) in the mid-1950s. Other authors have also attempted to evaluate these three areas of theory and to provide information about both McCarthy's supporters and the partisans of the John Birch Society.

AUTHORITARIANISM

Citing the work of Hodges, Graham, and Anderson,[18] Polsby argues that McCarthy's supporters were conformists and were likely to agree with statements to the effect that "people are out to cheat you." Presumably these characteristics are consistent with "the 'conventional' syndrome"[19] and its associated stereotypical behaviors, and with the suspiciousness with which authoritarians view the world, described as "world as jungle" by the authors of *The Authoritarian Personality.*[20] Polsby, however, notes that some presumably authoritarian segments of the population did not support McCarthy, and that despite the fact that in the county studied by Hodges *et al.* McCarthy's supporters were more anti-Semitic than those who did not support him, they were no more anti-Negro. Therefore these findings on conformity and authoritarianism are inconclusive, considering the high correlations we should expect to find between the F scale and the E scale, which are supposed to measure authoritarianism and ethnocentrism, respectively. Generally speaking, Polsby's data on authoritarianism are inadequate to test this particular hypothesis about McCarthy's supporters. Martin Trow's find-

[18]Harold M. Hodges, Jr., Charles Graham, and Philip Anderson, "A Sociological Analysis of McCarthy Supporters" (a paper delivered at the 52nd annual meeting of the American Sociological Society, Washington, D.C., August 1957), cited in Polsby, "McCarthyism," pp. 810–12.

[19]Adorno *et al., Authoritarian Personality,* p. 756.

[20]*Ibid.,* pp. 411–13.

ing that support for McCarthy and political intolerance were independent variables suggests that if authoritarianism is manifested by hostility to civil liberties (political intolerance), it was not an important factor in support for McCarthy—at least not in Bennington, Vermont.[21]

Raymond E. Wolfinger and his associates, in their study of the participants in an anticommunist school sponsored by Fred Schwarz's Christian Anti-Communism Crusade,[22] used Trow's scale of political tolerance to measure the relative tolerance of their Crusaders. When they controlled for education, they found that their more highly educated male respondents were slightly less tolerant and their less educated male respondents were somewhat more tolerant than Trow's group, but they hesitated to conclude that the Crusaders were as tolerant as Trow's index indicated because of the Crusaders' intolerance of the civil liberties of persons they believed to be communists.[23] They terminate their discussion of tolerance by stating: "It is safest to conclude that our sample's level of tolerance compared to the general population is an unknown quantity." However, Wolfinger's data at least suggest that the Crusaders were not extremely intolerant, and when their responses on the item "Communists should be allowed to speak on radio and television" are compared with responses to a very similar item from the Stouffer study, they appear to be only slightly more in agreement with this item than Stouffer's combined national cross-section samples of respondents. Thus, if advocating the suppression of free speech of communists is in any way related to overt authoritarianism, the Crusaders seem to be only slightly more authoritarian than the rest of the population, if the time gap between these two surveys is not so great as to make comparisons between them wholly invalid.[24] The Crusaders, on the other hand, had relatively more education than the Stouffer sample, and therefore should show greater political tolerance than a cross-section sample.

However, while authoritarianism does not seem to have been strongly manifested in the form of political intolerance measured by

[21]Trow, "Right-Wing Radicalism," p. 20.

[22]Raymond E. Wolfinger *et al.*, "America's Radical Right: Politics and Ideology," in *Ideology and Discontent*, ed. David E. Apter (New York: Free Press, Macmillan, 1964), pp. 262–93.

[23]*Ibid.*, p. 273.

[24]Samuel Stouffer, *Communism, Conformity, and Civil Liberties* (Gloucester, Mass.: Peter Smith, 1963), p. 41, and Wolfinger *et al.*, "America's Radical Right," p. 273. Stouffer asked if a communist should be allowed to speak in the respondent's community; Wolfinger *et al.*, if communists should be allowed to speak on radio and television. The percentage of each sample agreeing that they should be allowed to speak was identical: 27 percent.

opinion surveys, there is some evidence to suggest that supporters of McCarthy and of the John Birch Society are more authoritarian in terms of F scale scores than are persons who have not supported either the late senator or the contemporary organized right.

The first test of this question was made by the National Opinion Research Center in a survey conducted in June 1953, unfortunately overlooked by Polsby in his review of the polls dealing with McCarthy. Lipset, however, has analyzed the data from that survey (which included a five-item abbreviation of the F scale), and when the respondents were controlled for education, he was able to conclude that "there is a relationship between propensity to give 'authoritarian' responses and support of McCarthy within the three education groups."[25] This difference was particularly noticeable among college-educated respondents, among whom 85 percent of the highly authoritarian supported McCarthy and only 50 percent of the slightly authoritarian approved of him.[26] Table II.1, adapted from Lipset's analysis, shows the other differences clearly. Lipset notes that these data are possibly best interpreted only as indicating that authoritarianism is positively associated with support for McCarthy among the better educated group because of the fact that authoritarianism has been shown to vary inversely with educational level: the higher the educational level, the lower the score on scales of authoritarianism. Table II.1 shows, however, that even in the lower educational categories the relationship between support for McCarthy and high authoritarianism is very clear.

The evidence for a positive relationship between authoritarianism and support for the contemporary American right is somewhat less substantial than the data just cited concerning McCarthy. I have no knowledge of any national surveys that have included any F scale items and at the same time asked about support for the John Birch Society or any other formal rightist organization.[27] There is, however, one study by Ira Rohter which suggests a positive relationship between authoritarianism and members of a sample of radical rightists studied in the area of Eugene, Oregon.[28] Rightists in this sample were identified from published membership lists of the John Birch Society and from

[25]Lipset, "Three Decades," pp. 411–14.

[26]*Ibid.*, p. 414.

[27]Chap. 5 contains a discussion of a survey that includes F-scale items, and authoritarianism is shown to be modestly associated with support for Wallace.

[28]Ira S. Rohter, "Some Personal Needs Met by Becoming a Radical Rightist" (paper delivered at the Society for the Psychological Study of Social Issues Symposium on the Socialization and Recruitment of Right-Wing Activists at the annual meeting of the American Psychological Association, Chicago, September 4, 1965).

other public expressions of rightist ideology by persons in the area. The control group in this study was selected by evidence of some non-rightist public activity, such as writing letters to newspapers in support of issues not espoused by rightists, so that it is in no sense a representative sample of community residents.[29] Rohter's findings are derived from a series of scales that he developed for his survey instrument, and although no use was made of the F scale or any short form of it, a number of his scale items are taken from the full F scale. Two of his scales, the Free-Floating Hostility Scale and the Sense of Personal Powerlessness Scale,[30] employ a number of these items. The scores obtained on these two scales by persons ranging from low to high in rightist sentiment are shown in Table II.2. As the data from this table indicate, the higher the score on the radical rightist index, the higher the score on the hostility scale. Since this scale is the best test of measured authoritarianism presented by Rohter, it appears that authoritarianism is positively associated with a high score on Rohter's Index of Radical Rightism. Although the difference between the two lower and two higher groups on the rightist index is not so clear-cut on the personal powerlessness scale (which also had F scale items in it) as it is on the hostility scale, it is nevertheless statistically significant in the expected direction.[31]

[29]*Ibid.*, p. 4. Rohter's sample of rightists, once selected, scored very high on a radical-right index that neatly differentiated his rightists from his controls. His control group was probably more "liberal" than an actual random sample of the community would have been.

[30]*Ibid.*, pp. 12–13. The items on the Free-Floating Hostility Scale are as follows: "1. Sex crimes, such as rape and attacks on children, deserve more than mere imprisonment; such criminals ought to be publicly whipped or worse." Compare with the following item from the F scale: "Sex crimes, such as rape and attacks on children, deserve more than mere imprisonment; such criminals ought to be publicly whipped or worse" (Adorno *et al., Authoritarian Personality*, p. 257). "2. There is hardly anything lower than a person who does not feel a great love, gratitude, and respect for his parents." Compare the same item from the F scale (Adorno *et al., Authoritarian Personality*, p. 255). "3. Homosexuals are hardly better than criminals and ought to be severely punished." Compare the same item from the F scale (Adorno *et al., Authoritarian Personality*, p. 255). The items from the Sense of Personal Powerlessness Scale are as follows: "1. Of all the different philosophies which exist in this world, there is probably only one which is correct. 2. There is usually only one right way to do anything. 3. People can be divided into two distinct classes: the weak and the strong" (compare with, the same item from the F scale [Adorno *et al., Authoritarian Personality*, p. 256]). "4. You can classify almost all people as either honest or crooked." Thus, four items from these two scales are taken directly from the F scale. The Free-Floating Hostility Scale has a Kuder-Richardson coefficient of internal consistency of +.89, the Sense of Personal Powerlessness Scale a coefficient of internal consistency of +.77.

[31]Rohter, "Personal Needs," pp. 12–13.

TABLE II.1

Relationships Between Attitudes Toward McCarthy Committee and Scores on Authoritarian Personality Scale Within Educational Groupings

(NORC, June 1953)

	Attitudes Toward McCarthy Committee		
	Approve	*Disapprove*	*Don't Know*
Grammar school			
High authoritarianism	56%	14%	30%
Medium authoritarianism	57	14	29
Low authoritarianism	45	16	39
High school			
High authoritarianism	78	10	12
Medium authoritarianism	65	16	19
Low authoritarianism	61	24	15
College			
High authoritarianism	85	10	5
Medium authoritarianism	66	20	14
Low authoritarianism	50	39	11

Adapted from Seymour Martin Lipset, "Three Decades of the Radical Right," in *The Radical Right,* ed. Daniel Bell (New York: Doubleday Anchor Books, 1964).

The meaning of these data is severely compromised, however, by the fact that Rohter's control group was selected from persons who were openly active in public affairs and issues. Many studies have shown that such persons are usually more highly educated and conscious of civil liberties than the remainder of the population.[32] Furthermore, while 42 percent of Rohter's control group fell into his category of high social status, only 27 percent of his rightists fell into this class. Additionally, 77 percent of his nonrightist control group were in high-level occupational roles and had graduated from college; some of them had also attended graduate school. Only 59 percent of his rightist sample met these criteria. A similar pattern prevailed in his middle occupational group.[33] Since authoritarianism is inversely correlated with advanced education and high social status, the fact that persons with these characteristics were disproportionately represented in Rohter's control group suggests that the meaning of these data on the question

[32]Stouffer, *Communism,* and Lila Sussmann, *Dear F.D.R.: A Study of Political Letter Writing* (Totowa, N.J.: Bedminster Press, 1963).
[33]Rohter, "Personal Needs," pp. 2, 5.

of authoritarianism is, in the absence of an analysis controlled for education and socioeconomic status, highly ambiguous.

And so the evidence offered in support of the hypothesis that authoritarianism is positively associated with support for either McCarthy or the contemporary American right is somewhat inconclusive. The best support for the hypothesis comes from Lipset's analyses of the June 1953 poll of the National Opinion Research Center. Finally, the findings of Trow and Wolfinger—that support for either McCarthy or the contemporary right is not definitely related to political intolerance—suggest that if rightists are authoritarians, they do not invariably manifest their authoritarianism in the form of unusually intolerant political attitudes. In my opinion, then, the hypothesis is unproved, and some extremely careful, large-scale survey research will be needed to test it before the utility of authoritarianism as a causal variable in the formation of rightist political and social movements can be demonstrated.

MASS SOCIETY THEORIES: STATUS DISCREPANCY AND STATUS ANXIETY

The two theories that have been most influential in empirical research on the contemporary right are based on two rather different propositions that center on the influence of social status and social mobility as causal variables in the production of rightists' beliefs. Broadly speaking, these two ideas are products of the concept of status politics, a condition thought to be the result of a high rate of economic expansion in which social and occupational mobility is much greater than in times of depression. Great mobility, whether upward or downward, is seen to be the source of anxiety and frustration, both because of its potentially disruptive effects on interpersonal relations and be-

TABLE II.2

Comparison of High and Low Scores on Radical Rightist Index
with High Scores on Free-Floating Hostility Scale
and Sense of Personal Powerlessness Scale

Radical Rightist Index	High Scores on Free-Floating Hostility Scale	High Scores on Powerlessness Scale
I (low)	13%	24%
II	17	28
III	32	40
IV (high)	39	35

cause high rates of mobility are presumably sources of insecurity as a result of the great changes in status of many persons who have not been socialized to play their new roles with conviction or success.

The first proposition deriving from these ideas is status discrepancy. Formally stated, status discrepancy is the condition of an *individual,* and by extension of a *social group,* that possesses one or more of the components of a social-status location but none of the other requisite characteristics of that status location. For example, consider a newly rich manufacturer who never went beyond the sixth grade and continues to do manual labor in his shop from time to time. Here the discrepant variable is income. In other cases, education or occupation may be discrepant, depending, of course, on the circumstances of the particular case. The logic of status discrepancy theory is that persons who have incongruent levels of the three central sociological components of status—income, occupation, and education—are likely to develop attitudes favorable to the right, because the right is the organized and visible segment of the society that is most radical in attacking the established political and social power structures within the system while at the same time affirming the importance of individualism and the legitimacy of hoarding one's money for oneself. Persons lacking status congruity are presumed to harbor resentments against the established elite sectors of the society, whose existence somehow shows them up as pretenders, *nouveaux riches,* interlopers, phonies, or bumpkins. The Texas oilman is the archetype of this sort of individual. Note that in this formulation, status discrepancy is a strictly structural proposition, referring to *objective discrepancies* between three components of social status: occupation, education, and income. What evidence is there to support or reject this notion?[34]

In Martin Trow's study of Bennington, status discrepancy was not found to be a very important characteristic of McCarthy's supporters. In fact, education, not social status or status discrepancy, was of far greater influence in the attenuation of support for the Senator. Trow found that college-educated manual workers—a clearly discrepant group—"by and large did not respond to McCarthy's appeals."[35] Furthermore, intergenerational social mobility, both upward and downward, was of less importance than a respondent's present occupation in determining whether or not he supported McCarthy.[36] Trow did not, however, measure the intragenerational mobility of McCarthy's supporters.

[34]See Lipset, "Three Decades"; Daniel Bell, "The Dispossessed"; and Richard Hofstadter, "The Pseudo-Conservative Revolt"; all in *Radical Right,* ed. Bell.
[35]Trow, "Right-Wing Radicalism," p. 75.
[36]*Ibid.,* p. 106.

Lipset cites a study by Robert Sokol which, he says, "seem[s] to confirm the hypotheses presented in the original essays [in *The New American Right*] concerning stratification factors and McCarthyism."[37.] Sokol used a measure of "felt status inconsistency," however, and as we shall see, *feelings* of status inconsistency are not necessarily comparable to *objective* status discrepancies, and therefore may not be considered as confirming the theory of status discrepancy—although they do give some support to the status anxiety hypothesis, which will be discussed in detail below. This evidence does not in any way confirm the status discrepancy theory.

In a test of the status discrepancy hypothesis, Wolfinger's Crusaders were found to "have at least as much status stability as the comparison group. Furthermore, within [their] sample, the status-stable businessmen and professionals were *more likely* than the upwardly mobile ones to choose conservative positions on every attitude measure."[38]

Extending this concept into measures of relative deprivation, Polsby, in his study of support for McCarthy, found that lower-class, poorly educated, and Catholic respondents in the surveys he reviewed were more likely to support McCarthy than people in other social groupings.[39] And Trow also found disproportionate support for McCarthy among poorly educated manual workers.[40] Polsby confirms some of the predictions made by the authors of *The New American Right* concerning groups with "deprived" status, but these findings and those reported by Trow and Wolfinger suggest that the status discrepancy hypothesis has little utility in explaining either support for McCarthy or the behavior of the more contemporary group of rightists studied by Wolfinger.

However, one recent study[41] by Gary Rush does provide some weak support for the status discrepancy hypothesis. Rush employed Gerhard Lenski's status crystallization model to divide his sample into two groups of persons with low and high status consistency based on the level of agreement among the three objective criteria of social status.[42] (Status crystallization is the condition of balanced or congruent components of social status; it is in every respect equivalent to the

[37]Robert Sokol, "Rank Inconsistency and McCarthyism: An Empirical Test" (unpublished paper, n.d.), cited in Lipset, "Three Decades," p. 403.

[38]Wolfinger, "America's Radical Right," p. 278 (my italics).

[39]Polsby, "McCarthyism," p. 816.

[40]Trow, "Right-Wing Radicalism," p. 79.

[41]Gary B. Rush, "Status Consistency and Right-Wing Extremism," *American Sociological Review*, 32, no. 1 (February 1967): 86–92.

[42]Gerhard E. Lenski, "Status Crystallization: A Non-Vertical Dimension of Social Status," *American Sociological Review*, 19, no. 3 (August 1954): 724–33.

term "status congruity" used by Wolfinger.) He then compared the responses of these two groups of respondents on a number of items designed to measure right-wing extremism. He found confirmation at the .06 level of confidence for his hypothesis that "individuals characterized by status inconsistency are more likely to be right-wing extremists in their political attitudes than individuals who are characterized by status consistency, when the invalidating effects of status differences in occupation, income, and education are controlled."[43]

However, it seems that either right-wing extremists are heavily over-represented in Rush's sample or his measure of extremism is not sufficiently discriminating, because he reports that 21 percent of the sample was classified as extremist, a figure far higher than is suggested by any of the national surveys that have included questions that might be used to ascertain the extent of support for extremist groups in the American population. Rush states that "holding attitudes consistent with the extreme right ideology"[44] is the equivalent (for his sample) of being an extremist.[45] Nevertheless, Rush's data in their published form do not permit extended secondary analysis.[46]

Rohter also attempted to evaluate both the status anxiety and status discrepancy hypotheses and found that the rightists in his sample were, on the whole, more downwardly mobile than his control group, although among high-status rightists upward mobility was greater than among his high-status controls. He also found that "rightists in the higher and middle-status occupations have less education than non-rightists in the same situation." This finding, however, is ambiguous, again because of the characteristics of his nonrightist control group and because relative mobility is not really a direct test of status discrepancy.[47]

STATUS ANXIETY

Status anxiety, while possibly resulting from actual status discrepancy, is not equivalent to it because it substitutes perceived, felt, or

[43]Rush, "Status Consistency," p. 90.

[44]*Ibid.*, p. 89.

[45]See Trow, "Right-Wing Radicalism," and Wolfinger, "America's Radical Right."

[46]Rush remarks, "Low educational status might be more closely related to right-wing extremism than differences in either occupational or income statuses" (p. 91). This is consistent with the findings of Trow and Stouffer concerning the increasing support for civil liberties that accompanies increased levels of education, and suggests that political tolerance is, in fact, an important part of Rush's attitudinal measures of extremism.

[47]Rohter, "Personal Needs," p. 18.

reported feelings of status discrepancy for any objective measures of it. Typically such anxiety is measured by an item that asks the respondent if he feels that his neighbors give him as much respect as he feels he deserves, a somewhat doubtful measure of status-relevant behavior.

In the study by Sokol mentioned briefly above and reported by Lipset, perceived status discrepancies were found to be related to support for McCarthy:

The more strain [i.e., status anxiety], the greater will be the tendency to be a McCarthy supporter; with 62 percent of the high-strain men being pro-McCarthy, in contrast with 47 percent of those feeling a little strain and 39 percent of those without any concern about the relative ranks of their statuses.[48]

Rohter's tests of status anxiety are much more sophisticated than most and are based on three items that measure perceived acceptance in the community, perception of the society as closed or open, and expressed belief in the existence of a small, closed group of elites in the respondent's community who exclude him from any social advancement. The rightists' responses to the first two of these items were found to be significantly different from the nonrightists' in the direction confirming status anxiety. Rightist responses to the last item were also found to be significantly different from those of nonrightists when the rightist respondents were controlled for status losers and status gainers; the status losers significantly more often agreed with that item.[49]

Rohter's data, then, give some further confirmation to the theories of both status discrepancy and status anxiety. But it is perhaps appropriate to conclude this section of the review of the literature relevant to these two major sociological theories of the right with Rohter's final summary of his findings:

In this paper I have examined three types of variables, dealing with status anxieties, value concerns, and personality.... As we have seen, while the status anxiety variables conform to expectations, they nevertheless produced the weakest relationships, while value concerns and personality variables have produced overwhelming differences between Rightists and non-Rightists....[50]

Nevertheless, I shall argue in the last chapter of this study that status anxiety, broadly defined, is an important causal variable in the production of right-wing extremism.

[48]Sokol, "Rank Inconsistency," p. 403.
[49]Rohter, "Personal Needs," pp. 20–21.
[50]*Ibid.*

INTERNATIONAL INVOLVEMENT AND
EXOGENOUS VALUE STRAIN

In addition to the ideas about the etiology of rightism that have been drawn from the mass society and authoritarian studies, Talcott Parsons and Samuel Lubbell have advanced the theory that the increasing international involvement of the United States in the period following World War II was in large part responsible for the body of anticommunist, aggressive isolationist, and neo-populist opinion that supposedly united around McCarthy.[51] Parsons says: "My thesis . . . is that the strains of the international situation have impinged on a society undergoing important changes which have themselves been sources of strain, with the effect of imposing one kind of strain on another."[52] Parsons argues that the intersection of these two sets of exogenous and endogenous value strains resulted in two types of protective or compensatory behavior: on the one hand in a mobilization of patriotism and loyalty among the American population through pressure to "subordinate private interests to public interests,"[53] and on the other hand in the designation of a scapegoat or cultural demon—the Communists —who could be blamed for the anxieties, stresses, and uncertainties that presumably were present among the population in postwar America as a result of the cold war and the associated threat of nuclear exchange. Lubbell argues that support for McCarthy arose among persons disenchanted with the practice of limited war in Korea and those who had opposed American entry into World War II.[54]

In his summary of these two suggestions, Nelson Polsby concludes that support for McCarthy should therefore have come from "people of German extraction . . . isolationists and . . . those who preferred dramatic activity to patience in the conduct of foreign affairs."[55] Limited support for these hypotheses was obtained by Lubbell[56] and by Hodges, Graham, and Anderson,[57] who report that German-Americans were in fact disproportionately favorable to McCarthy, and that those of their respondents who were opposed to foreign involvements, such as the Korean conflict and foreign aid, were also more likely to favor

[51]Parsons, "Social Strains," pp. 209–29, 231–38; and Samuel Lubbell, *The Future of American Politics,* 2nd ed. (Garden City, N.Y.: Doubleday, 1956).

[52]Parsons, "Social Strains," p. 217.

[53]*Ibid.*

[54]Samuel Lubbell, *The Revolt of the Moderates* (New York: Harper, 1956), p. 268.

[55]Polsby, "McCarthyism," p. 810.

[56]Lubbell, *Revolt.*

[57]Hodges *et al.,* "McCarthy Supporters," pp. 810–12.

McCarthy.[58] Polsby, however, dismisses the importance of this theory by pointing out that the stressful historical circumstances surrounding the postwar years "existed for everyone, and, save in the case of the relatively small German-American group, the hypothesis does not explain, for the purpose of assessing his political possibilities at any time, where in the population most of McCarthy's supporters could have been located."[59] This, I believe, is a too hasty interpretation of the influence on and importance of foreign affairs for the American right. Data that have been collected and analyzed since 1960 show that rightists seem to be extraordinarily concerned about foreign affairs and to hold both hostile and somewhat isolationist attitudes toward the Soviet Union and other communist nations. That is, their opposition to communism takes an isolationist form, even though they express great hostility to communist nations and therefore might be presumed to advocate aggressive policies toward them. Furthermore, isolationism in one form or another has been consistently found to be a component of American rightist opinion since the 1920s. Lipset, for example, found a weak but consistently isolationist pattern of responses from pro-McCarthy respondents in a number of national surveys he analyzed in 1962.[60] And anticommunist isolationism was also characteristic of Wolfinger's Crusaders; 37 percent of them agreed with the statement "The United States should have nothing to do with Russia." Only 17 percent of the respondents in Stouffer's national samples gave the same response.[61] Rohter also found the rightists in his sample to be extremely dogmatic in their views on communism and Russia. Among rightists scoring at the extreme end of his index of radical rightism (IV), 68 percent gave a highly dogmatic response. Only 27 percent of those in the next lowest (III) category of radical rightism responded in this fashion.[62] His scale was made up of items that appear to measure both approval of isolationism and undifferentiated perceptions of communist nations.[63]

While these notions have not yet been thoroughly explored, they have received limited confirmation in the data concerning the importance of isolationism to many rightists from the McCarthy period onward. Furthermore, these ideas and those developed by Polsby and Wolfinger have drawn attention to the possible significance of political

---

[58]Polsby, "McCarthyism," pp. 810–11.
[59]*Ibid.*
[60]Lipset, "Three Decades," p. 409. He notes that "perhaps [it is] more significant . . . that these relationships are so weak. . . ."
[61]Wolfinger *et al.,* "America's Radical Right," p. 271; Stouffer, *Communism.*
[62]Rohter, "Personal Needs," p. 9.
[63]*Ibid.*

variables in explanations of rightist behavior, and, as we shall see, political variables are perhaps the single most significant set of discriminators isolated thus far in empirical research on the American right.

THE IMPLICATIONS OF PRESENT EMPIRICAL KNOWLEDGE FOR THEORY CONSTRUCTION AND A SUMMARY OF SIGNIFICANT FINDINGS

The Supporters of Senator McCarthy

Both Lipset and Polsby have given extended attention to the poll data that might identify the ethnic and other social groups in the population that gave disproportionately great support to Senator McCarthy.[64] On the basis of their analyses of relevant polls, the groups appearing in Table II.3 may with some certainty be said to have been among those providing this support. The picture that emerges from this evidence is one of a large number of relatively lower status occupa-

TABLE II.3

Ethnic and Demographic Social Groupings Giving
Disproportionate Support to Senator McCarthy

Groups Showing High Support in Two or More Polls	Groups Showing High Support in One Uncontradicted Poll
Catholics	Republicans
Less educated	Manual workers
Lower class	Polish Catholics
Farmers	Elderly
Irish*	New Englanders
	Older American Protestant families

Adapted from Seymour Martin Lipset, "Three Decades of the Radical Right," in *The Radical Right,* ed. Daniel Bell (New York: Doubleday Anchor Books, 1964), and Nelson W. Polsby, "Towards an Explanation of McCarthyism," in *Politics and Social Life,* ed. Nelson W. Polsby, Robert A. Dentler, and Paul Smith (Boston: Houghton Mifflin, 1963).
*Polsby reports that the Irish did not contribute disproportionate support, but Lipset, in a reanalysis of Polsby's data, shows that in fact the Irish were overrepresented in Polsby's sample.

[64]Lipset, "Three Decades," pp. 403–8, and Polsby, "McCarthyism," p. 814.

tional, ethnic, and religious groups and a few loosely defined hetero-geneous social groups, such as Republicans, farmers, and the elderly.

Trow's findings concerning the occupations of McCarthy's sup-porters in Bennington, while not, of course, based on a national sample survey, indicate that small businessmen were more likely to support McCarthy than any other group in his sample; and Lipset has demon-strated that small businessmen were the group in the middle class who were most likely to give support to McCarthy, thus confirming Trow's finding with two national sample surveys.[65] The bulk of support for McCarthy, however, came from blue-collar workers and farmers. These groups share two common characteristics: They have a relatively high proportion of persons who are economically marginal and, relative to the middle classes, have more marginal political attachments.

The principal psychological or attitudinal characteristic that Trow found to be associated with support for McCarthy was nineteenth-century liberalism—that is, clusters of persons who had negative atti-tudes to *both* large-scale business organizations and labor unions. Trow found that his McCarthy supporters were much more likely to hold such attitudes than were any of three other groups of persons with different political orientations.[66] Finally, authoritarianism was given some limited support as an explanatory variable of support for McCarthy in the study reported by Lipset.

Polsby was one of the first social scientists to introduce an elementary but very fruitful hypothesis into the debate over who sup-ported McCarthy. He presents very impressive evidence that McCarthy received his greatest support among Republicans. For example, among persons who were favorable to McCarthy in a Gallup survey conducted in April 1954, the mean percentage of pro-Republican responses to four measures of party sympathy was 53 percent, pro-Democratic responses amounted to 26 percent, and undecided members of the electorate gave pro-Republican responses 11 percent of the time.[67]

Lipset also confirms Polsby's finding in an analysis of the 1952 election study conducted by the Survey Research Center of the Uni-versity of Michigan. The distribution of pro-McCarthy responses by party identification among respondents in that survey was: strong Democrats, 10 percent; weak Democrats, 9 percent; independent Demo-

[65]Trow, "Right-Wing Radicalism," and Lipset, "Three Decades."

[66]Trow, "Right-Wing Radicalism," p. 35.

[67]Polsby, "McCarthyism," p. 819, recomputed from data provided in Table X. The test of Republicanism used by Polsby is very rigorous, requiring both a self-expressed party identification and agreement with three questionnaire items concerning party loyalty, voting behavior, and attitude toward party.

crats, 8 percent; independents, 12 percent; independent Republicans, 12 percent; weak Republicans, 12 percent; and strong Republicans, 25 percent.[68] Lipset argues that despite the high levels of Republicanism shown to be associated with support for McCarthy, there is evidence to suggest that he may have been the cause of party migration (from Democratic to Republican) by persons who favored him, thus possibly confounding the meaning of the findings from the 1954 Gallup survey and the 1952 election study.[69] Lipset's evidence, however, is by no means convincing, because it rests on reported shifts in vote intention between 1948 and 1952 without employing controls for strength of party identification among the supposed migrants—an extremely important variable in any analysis of voting shifts. And as Lipset's own analysis shows, it was the *strong* Republicans who were most likely to be supporters of McCarthy. Because of this fact and also because of the much higher levels of vote switching that occur among persons with weak party identifications, any test of possible party migration based on voting should differentiate among degrees of party identification.[70]

Furthermore, Lipset shows that it was education, not party preference, that was "the most important single attribute associated with support of McCarthy," and he presents a table (Table II.4) to substantiate this claim. Although, as an inspection of this table will show, education was indeed strongly related to support for McCarthy, the table also demonstrates that the effects of party identification were also very strong, amounting to very substantial differences between Republicans and Democrats at every educational level.

What relationships to theory have these demographic, political, and attitudinal findings about support for McCarthy? It seems clear that support for McCarthy was inversely related to education, and that a low level of education and a Republican party preference—not mobility, perceived or objective status discrepancies, or exogenous value strains—were the two most influential factors in the production of support for McCarthy. In Stouffer's *Communism, Conformity, and Civil Liberties,* a high level of education was found to be very strongly associated with support for civil liberties and tolerance of noncon-

[68]Lipset, "Three Decades," p. 396. Republicans were also far less likely to be anti-McCarthy.

[69]*Ibid.*

[70]This survey was not national, but was conducted in eleven states and had an extremely large sample, 9,852. Lipset says, "There is no good reason to assume that . . . variations . . . within these eleven states were not characteristic of reactions to McCarthy generally" (*ibid.,* p. 399); nevertheless, there is no good reason to assume that they *were* characteristic, especially since no southern states were included in the sample.

TABLE II.4

Support for McCarthy by Educational Level and Party Preference, 1954
(Percentage Differences Between Approval and Disapproval of McCarthy)

	Party Identification		
Education	*Democrat*	*Independent*	*Republican*
Graduate school	−59%	−44%	−28%
College	−44	−24	−19
·Vocational school	−41	−20	−19
High school	−27	− 8	− 5
Grammar school	−18	− 8	+ 6

Source: Seymour Martin Lipset, "Three Decades of the Radical Right,"
in *The Radical Right,* ed. Daniel Bell (New York: Doubleday Anchor
Books, 1964), p. 398.

formity, a finding that not surprisingly suggests that support for Mc-
Carthy, a person conspicuously unconcerned about civil liberties, came
from that segment of the society—the less educated—that was also less
tolerant of nonconformity and less likely to support civil liberties than
were persons with moderate or high levels of formal education.[71]

The Supporters of the Contemporary Right

In view of these findings on the relationship between education
and support for McCarthy, it is somewhat surprising to find that
education was *positively* associated with early support for the John
Birch Society and other contemporary rightist groups. In three polls
conducted in 1962 and cited by Lipset, education was found to be high
among those persons who both supported and opposed the society. By
the end of 1964, when the vast majority of the population was aware
of the organization, the bulk of its supporters came from the middle
educational levels, with the greatest levels of approval coming from
persons with high school diplomas or from those who had completed
nine or more grades and had acquired some additional formal training
of one sort or another. In late 1964, college-educated persons were
least likely to be neutral in their position on the society and to be
most informed about it (only 3.1 percent did not know of the society).
Only 5 percentage points separated those who supported the society

[71]Stouffer, *Communism,* p. 146.

from those opposing it among these highly educated respondents, indicating that a high level of education is no insurance against support of an organization that has received extremely large amounts of negative publicity focused on the supposedly antidemocratic, fascist, and intolerant nature of its beliefs and its members (see Table II.5).

Wolfinger also discovered that his Crusaders were four times more likely to have college educations than were white residents of the San Francisco Bay area in general, and Rohter found that 59 percent of his sample of rightists had college educations.[72] The occupational groups that appear to have been heavily overrepresented among those supporting the Birch Society were farmers, professional and technical workers, and the retired.[73]

Republican party identification in conjunction with a high level of education was apparently the best predictor of support for the Birch Society and the Christian Anti-Communism Crusade. The Crusaders, even when controlled for social class, were heavily Republican: for every Democrat in Wolfinger's sample there were eight Republicans.[74] Lipset found that it was among high-status Republicans that the John Birch Society received its greatest support: 18 percent of these respondents in a January 1962 California poll supported the society, middle-status Republicans followed with 8 percent supporting it, and only 6 percent of low-status Republicans supported the society. Even at the lowest status levels, however, Republicans were at least twice as likely as Democrats to support the society. At every status level Democrats gave responses favorable to the Birch Society only 3 percent of the time, although high-status Democrats were more likely to be opposed to the society than others of their party.[75]

Rohter and Wolfinger also found evidence that religious fundamentalism and value-oriented protests against secularism, "moral decline," and to some extent bureaucratization of society were part of the complex of factors that differentiate contemporary rightists from others in the population.

One of the more promising integrations of the findings on support for McCarthy and the contemporary American right has been provided by Wolfinger. He suggests that the right is the result of an absence

[72]Wolfinger *et al.*, "America's Radical Right," p. 268, and Rohter, "Personal Needs," p. 5.
[73]Lipset, "Three Decades," pp. 422–30, and Wolfinger *et al.*, "America's Radical Right," p. 268.
[74]According to data supplied to me by Professor Wolfinger, there were 204 Republicans and 25 Democrats in his sample.
[75]Lipset, "Three Decades," p. 431.

TABLE II.5

Support for John Birch Society by Educational Level
(Of Respondents Having an Opinion)

Education	1962 Gallup Poll (58% with an Opinion)		Education	1962 California Poll (62% with an Opinion)		Education	1964 SRC Poll (79% with an Opinion)	
	Pro	Con		Pro	Con		Pro	Con
Grade school	13%	13%	Grade school	4%	7%	Grade school	7.9%	12.8%
High school	57	53	High school	34	43	9 + years tech. school	42.1	30.7
College	30	34	Some college	26	23	High school	34.9	37.1
			3 + years college	36	27	College and above	15.1	19.5

Adapted from Seymour Martin Lipset, "Three Decades of the Radical Right," in *The Radical Right*, ed. Daniel Bell (New York: Doubleday Anchor Books, 1964), pp. 427–30, and the 1964 election study of the Survey Research Center, University of Michigan.

of strong party organizations, particularly Republican organizations, and that

where the Radical Right flourishes, political party organizations are weak and lack continuity. Control of a major party is a major inducement to right-wing activity in a number of states. But where party organizations are strong, where established leaders have formidable resources for protecting their positions from challengers, and where the rewards for political action run more toward tangible benefits than ideological satisfaction, the difficulty of taking over the party discourages potential right-wing activists. . . .[76]

This formulation of the problem not only has the advantage of accounting for the empirical findings that have been gathered thus far on the contemporary right, but also fits very well with the theory of political marginality advanced by the authors of *The American Voter*[77] in their discussion of agrarian political behavior. A conspicuous feature of much of the political activity in rural and agricultural areas of the United States was the alternation of passive and marginal political involvements on the part of most farmers with explosive and often violent political protests, often taking the form of regionally successful third-party movements.[78]

In a very persuasive argument, these authors suggest that this pattern of behavior is best explained by three factors: first, the existence of an elite organized around an ideology that may take various forms but is largely irrelevant to the members of any potential mass base of support for a social movement; second, the existence of a nonideological and politically marginal mass, which is unaccustomed to working through party organizations in order to meet its economic needs or secure resolution of its grievances; finally, an economic decline that affects the mass base sufficiently so that the elites are able to mobilize it for a short time, without, however, exacting any long-term party commitments from it; for as soon as the immediate economic stress is lifted from the mass, it characteristically reverts to its former pattern of political apathy. Of central importance in this explanation of the origins of agricultural protest movements is the absence of strong party ties among the elites and the mass base of the movement. In the absence of these bonds, third parties and large-scale pressure groups, such as the Nonpartisan League, the Grange, and the Populist (People's) party have emerged; and if we substitute symbolic and value-related

[76]Wolfinger *et al.,* "America's Radical Right," p. 287.

[77]Angus Campbell *et al., The American Voter* (New York: Wiley, 1960), pp. 402–40.

[78]This theory will be discussed in greater detail in chap. 5.

discontent for the economic factors that precipitated the agrarian protests, the movement led by George Wallace in 1968 appears to be very similar in social composition to the agrarian revolts.

GOLDWATER AND WALLACE:
THE RIGHT IN NATIONAL POLITICS

If this is an acceptable comparison and we can begin to extrapolate from the evidence just reviewed to contemporary rightist movements at the electoral level, then one is led to the question of the relationship between the Wallace and Goldwater movements, and specifically to the degree of fit between the Goldwater supporters (who were, relatively speaking, privileged middle to upper middle class in background) and the role assigned to the activating elite by the authors of *The American Voter*. Was there a substantial migration of the early supporters of Senator Goldwater to the ranks of Wallace's American Independent party, and if so, did they attain leadership positions? Can the AIP look forward to a period of growth and consolidation much like the People's party, the American Protective Association, and the Know-Nothings? The formation of the AIP and the success of its candidate in the South and in some urban areas in the North suggests that the development of a national political apparatus with totalitarian overtones is certainly not impossible within contemporary American society. The replacement of economic expansion by recession or depression, with concomitant disruption of the economic security of the working and marginal middle class, could, in my opinion, enable this apparatus, or one very much like it, to transform the existing symbolic and newly emerging economic grievances of this segment of the society into political power at the national level. At this writing it seems possible that the precipitous decline of the stock market and the rise in unemployment and inflation may, unfortunately, provide an opportunity to test this idea.

However, I do not anticipate the survival of the AIP as a party with enduring influence on electoral politics and I do not find it easy to imagine the formation of an enduring coalition between the conservative Republicans who supported Barry Goldwater in 1964 and the forces backing George Wallace in 1968, even though some ideological similarities between these groups do exist at the higher level of leadership. Briefly, this prognosis is founded upon my opinion that by taking his cause into the bleak environment of American third parties, Wallace has left behind in both the Democratic and Republican parties many thousands of ideologues and near ideologues who share his general concern with federal power, states' rights, and, in many cases, racism. But in the Republican party, at least, it is precisely these persons who have overlaid their ideological preferences with strong devotion to the party. My impression is that without a massive shift of such persons to the cause of a third party such as the AIP, the new party will founder for lack of guidance and support from the necessary critical mass of local political elites.

CHAPTER III

Demographic and Social Status
Correlates of Support
for Goldwater and Johnson
in the Election of 1964

BARRY GOLDWATER ran the most conservative campaign in recent Republican party history and was widely perceived (and advertised) as a conservative and often (incorrectly, I believe) as a right-wing extremist. It therefore seems reasonable to assume that he attracted the vast majority of conservatives and rightists to his cause in 1964. There is every indication that he received very strong support from members of conservative and superpatriotic voluntary associations. In his acceptance speech in San Francisco he seemed to welcome the support of extremists.

In selecting as the major dependent variable of my analysis of the Goldwater movement those persons who supported Goldwater before he was nominated for the presidency and who intended to (and in all probability did) vote for him in the national election of 1964, I am, of course, acting on the basis of a series of assumptions that ought to be made explicit at this point. In constructing an analytic group based upon candidate preference and vote intention, I am emphasizing *operational* conservatism. That is, I view early support for Goldwater's candidacy as prima facie evidence of conservative behavior. And since I believe that behavioral measures are, generally speaking, more powerful predictors of patterns of human behavior than are attitudinal assessments, selection of this set of measures yields a group for analysis which is, in my estimation, more likely than not to provide insight into the behavior of conservatives in areas other than their candidate preferences and vote intentions in 1964. Nevertheless, it will certainly be argued that I have left many conservatives out of my consideration, because there were substantial numbers of these people who voted for Johnson because of traditional Democratic party loyalty or who did not vote at all. My response to this is twofold. While undoubtedly such persons existed in 1964, there was also a large amount of vote-switching on the part of conservative Democratic elites (for example, George Wallace, Sam Yorty, Lester Maddox, Strom Thurmond) who supported Goldwater at the national level and Democrats at the state and local levels. These elites publicly announced that they intended to support Goldwater. This pattern was followed by many southern voters, who gave Goldwater his only electoral votes outside of his home state of Arizona. Additionally, defection from the Republican ticket was so high that some observers felt it signaled a realignment of partisan identification. Thus it may be argued that the level of ideological polarization among the politically sophisticated segments of the electorate (and in the South among much of the electorate in general) was sufficiently great in 1964 so that we may expect that the vast majority of attitudinal and operational conservatives migrated to Goldwater and liberals to Johnson, irrespective of their normal partisan identification.

Another somewhat more direct test of the adequacy of this assumption can be devised from the Survey Research Center's 1964 election study. In an early series of attempts to isolate attitudinal conservatives and rightists, I followed Lipset's practice in his essay "Three Decades of the Radical Right."[1] Selecting from the data all respondents who rated the John Birch Society favorably (that is, who gave it a rating of 60 degrees or more in the feeling-thermometer measure discussed in the first chapter), I isolated a group of 127 pro-Birch respondents. Only a third of these persons (forty-three) were also early supporters of Senator Goldwater. This finding immediately brought into serious question both the adequacy of the simple pro-Birch–neutral–anti-Birch measure as an indicator of operational political conservatism, and also, of course, the assumption, often made by political pundits, that early support for Goldwater would produce nearly uniform support for the Birch Society.

There are a number of reasons why operational conservatives may not support groups like the John Birch Society. William F. Buckley, for

[1]Seymour Martin Lipset, "Three Decades of the Radical Right," in *The Radical Right,* ed. Daniel Bell (New York: Doubleday Anchor Books, 1964).

example, has staged a running attack on Robert Welch for years, and other prominent conservatives have denounced the Birch Society as irresponsible and harmful to the conservative cause. Nevertheless, some further examination of the differences between the pro-Birch, pro-Goldwater group and the pro-Birch, anti-Goldwater group seemed appropriate. Were many true conservatives actually being excluded by the use of the candidate-preference criterion for construction of the dependent variable?

The test employed was an assessment of these two groups' feelings about liberals and labor unions. Presumably, neither Birch supporters nor conservatives would be likely to exhibit great warmth of feeling for these groups; neutrality or antipathy seem more likely responses. The pro-Birch, pro-Goldwater group conformed to this expectation rather nicely: 74 percent of them rated liberals negatively (less than 50 degrees), and 61 percent also disliked labor unions. But the picture is quite different when we examine the attitudes of the remaining pro-Birch group. Only 28 percent of these persons disliked liberals; 32 percent were hostile to unions. Evidently there was a much higher degree of attitudinal consistency among the early pro-Goldwater, pro-Birch group.

It thus appeared that the more consistent rightists supported Goldwater much more often than any other candidate, and that the designation of a group as rightist on the basis of the simple pro-Birch measure would include a large number of persons who would be incorrectly classified. Thus, while the criterion of early support for Goldwater may have been weak relative to the use of a valid and reliable attitude scale as a means of separating attitudinally consistent and inconsistent rightists, it proved considerably more viable than the mere indication of support or opposition to the John Birch Society, which has been used by Lipset and others as a sufficient criterion for isolation of their analytic groups.

A consideration of the character and degree of constraint among the opinions, behaviors, and attitudes of Goldwater's supporters leads us to further questions: Was Goldwater's candidacy actually supported by a social movement of an extremist (that is to say radical) sort, or was support for Goldwater in fact a conservative political impulse? Was there sufficient constraint among the beliefs of Goldwater's supporters to justify us in considering them ideologues within a political setting that has been shown to harbor very few political animals of an ideological stripe? Finally, was Goldwaterism primarily an elite or a mass movement?

In his recent and valuable book on the McCarthy period, Michael

Rogin has pointed out the implications of these questions for analysis of the supporters of the late Senator McCarthy.[2] Attacking what he terms the pluralists'[3] (actually ex-radical pluralists') view of McCarthyism, which was in part based on their assumption of the equivalency of populism, progressivism, and McCarthyism as mass social movements (that is, antidemocratic and anti-institutional movements), Rogin accuses the ex-radicals of an elite bias—a bias that caused them to identify McCarthy with mass politics and to avoid consideration of institutional and elite support for his activities. It is unfortunately true that the same biases began almost immediately to color both the interpretations of the causes of the nomination and the analysis of the social support for Senator Goldwater.

Writing in the *Saturday Review,* for example, the late Professor Arthur Schlesinger, Sr., identified the appearance of Goldwater as a remanifestation of an extremism that pervaded the American Protective Association, the Know-Nothing party, the Ku Klux Klan, and the McCarthy movement.[4] Much of the liberal and not so liberal commentary on Goldwater not only reinforced this picture of the backers of Senator Goldwater as "nuts," "cranks," "neo-Nazis," and the like, but also, in a less pejorative vein, portrayed the senator and his supporters as irresponsible. "Responsibility" was a catchword among political commentators in 1964, and while we should not lose sight of the seeming lack of consistency (responsibility?) that governed the Republican candidate's conflicting pronouncements on foreign affairs and domestic policy, it does not follow that the supposed irresponsibility of an aspiring decision-maker should be employed as the single tool in an analysis of the persons who supported him.

Theodore H. White, author of *The Making of the President: 1964,* carries this form of analysis into the Republican party itself. White identifies the clash within the party over Goldwater's nomination as a conflict between the "eastern establishment" on the one hand and the "primitives" on the other. This differentiation, while convenient short-

---

[2] Michael P. Rogin, *The Intellectuals and McCarthy: The Radical Specter* (Cambridge: M.I.T. Press, 1967).

[3] *Ibid.* See especially Rogin's first chapter, "Radicalism and the Rational Society: The Pluralist View," pp. 9–31.

[4] Arthur M. Schlesinger, Sr., "Extremism in American Politics," *Saturday Review,* November 27, 1965, pp. 21–25. See also Lionel Lokos, *Hysteria 1964: The Fear Campaign Against Barry Goldwater* (New Rochelle, N.Y.: Arlington House, 1967), for an interesting collection of articles in which Goldwater was described as a fascist, Nazi, racist, etc. Lokos' volume is a postcampaign pro-Goldwater tract attempting to "set the record straight." Nevertheless, it is an interesting record of one important aspect of the 1964 campaign.

hand and far less disparaging in intent than the Schlesinger comparison, nevertheless points to the same general conclusions that Rogin and others have shown to be the conceptual downfall of the ex-radical pluralists: the assertion that American rightist politics are practiced primarily by unsocialized political actors lacking either the prerequisites or the stability to be trusted with political power and representing segments of the society that are, by definition, antidemocratic. As we shall see, there is evidence to suggest that Goldwater's supporters were not advocates of mass politics, were highly socialized political actors, came from normally conservative sectors of the society, and held social attitudes and policy preferences that may seem to many irresponsible and ill thought out but which were nevertheless held by persons with extraordinarily high levels of formal education and political involvement—conditions that are often associated, in the United States at least, with political responsibility. As we shall also see, there were very few persons in the mass public who favored Senator Goldwater's nomination; even among Republicans he was a fourth or fifth choice.

ECONOMIC STATUS AND SOCIAL CLASS

As I have suggested, Goldwater's early supporters were drawn from relatively high socioeconomic strata. Tables III.1 and III.2 report a number of findings about their income levels, years of formal education, and occupations compared with those of the other candidate-preference groups. As can be easily seen, the early pro-Goldwater group had about twice the percentage of college graduates as the later pro-Goldwater group and nearly three times as many, proportionally speaking, as the Johnson supporters. With 40.1 percent of their members in professional, technical, or managerial occupations and 60.7 percent in white-collar jobs of all types, they were more than 17 percentage points above their nearest rivals (the later supporters) on this dimension of social status. Their income level was, accordingly, relatively high. Seventeen percent of their members had family incomes of more than $15,000 per year, more than twice the national average, and an additional 22 percent reported incomes between $10,000 and $15,000.

How do these conditions compare with the respondents' self-reported social class, and what are their implications for the direction of social mobility experienced by them and by the other groups of respondents in the analysis?

The economic conditions of the various groups are not defined by these comparative data alone; other factors also enter in—personal

TABLE III.1

Education and Income of Candidate-Preference Groups, 1964

Education and Income	Early Goldwater Supporters		Later Goldwater Supporters		Johnson Supporters		Undecided and Other		Total	
	N	%	N	%	N	%	N	%	N	%
EDUCATION										
Grade school, some high school	24	22.9%	67	30.6%	378	45.4%	218	56.9%	687	44.6%
High school graduate	16	15.2	53	24.2	189	22.7	72	18.8	330	21.4
Some college	38	36.2	69	31.5	190	22.8	53	13.8	350	22.7
College graduate	27	25.7	30	13.7	76	9.1	40	10.4	173	11.2
Total	105	100.0%	219	100.0%	833	100.0%	383	100.0%	1,540	100.0%
INCOME*										
$ 0– 3,999	12	12.0%	49	23.2%	217	27.0%	142	39.4%	424	28.5%
4,000– 5,999	16	16.0	45	21.3	168	20.9	78	21.7	307	20.6
6,000– 7,499	11	11.0	22	10.4	136	16.9	45	12.5	214	14.4
7,500– 9,999	22	22.0	38	18.0	130	16.1	46	12.8	236	15.9
10,000–14,999	22	22.0	38	18.0	107	13.3	37	10.3	204	13.7
15,000 or more	17	17.0	19	9.0	47	5.8	12	3.3	103	6.9
Total	100	100.0%	211	100.0%	805	100.0%	360	100.0%	1,488	100.0%

*Expected combined family income.

TABLE III.2

Occupational Breakdown of Candidate-Preference Groups, 1964

Occupation*	Early Goldwater Supporters		Later Goldwater Supporters		Johnson Supporters		Undecided and Other		Total	
	N	%	N	%	N	%	N	%	N	%
WHITE COLLAR										
Professional and semiprofessional	12	11.7%	26	11.9%	77	9.4%	33	8.7%	148	9.7%
Self-employed business, artisans, manufacturers	29	28.4	45	20.6	123	15.0	48	12.7	245	16.1
Clerical and sales, buyers, agents, brokers, etc.	21	20.6	24	11.0	84	10.2	29	7.7	158	10.4
Total white collar	62	60.7%	95	43.5%	284	34.6%	110	29.1%	551	36.2%
BLUE COLLAR										
Skilled and semi-skilled	15	14.7%	41	18.8%	260	31.7%	119	31.5%	435	28.6%
Unskilled, service, farm laborers	2	2.0	11	5.0	79	9.6	38	10.0	130	8.6
Protective service	1	1.0	4	1.8	17	2.1	6	1.6	28	1.8
Total blue collar	18	17.7%	56	25.6%	356	43.4%	163	43.1%	593	39.0%
OTHER										
Farm operators	2	2.0%	18	8.3%	38	4.6%	17	4.5%	75	5.0%
Retired	17	16.7	35	16.1	101	12.3	55	14.6	208	13.7
Housewives	3	2.9	13	6.0	32	3.9	25	6.6	73	4.8
Unemployed	0	0.0	1	0.4	10	1.2	8	2.1	19	1.3
Total other	22	21.6%	67	30.8%	181	22.0%	105	27.8%	375	24.8%
Grand total	102	100.0%	218	100.0%	821	100.0%	378	100.0%	1,519	100.0%

*Head of household.

TABLE III.3

Level of Economic Satisfaction Among
Candidate-Preference Groups, 1964

	"Pretty Well Satisfied"		"More or Less Satisfied"		"Not Satisfied at All"		Total	
	N	%	N	%	N	%	N	%
Early Goldwater supporters	41	39.0%	54	51.4%	10	9.5%	105	100.0%
Later Goldwater supporters	111	50.7	79	36.1	29	13.2	219	100.0
Johnson supporters	387	46.6	318	38.3	125	15.1	830	100.0
Undecided and other	148	38.8	161	42.3	72	18.9	381	100.0
Total	687	43.8	612	42.0	236	14.2	1,535	100.0

economic advance or decline and the respondents' perception of their financial condition, both of which are at least partially independent of levels of real income. Interestingly enough, there is a pattern of somewhat greater economic dissatisfaction among Goldwater's early supporters than among his later backers or among Johnson partisans. Table III.3 gives the breakdown of responses to a question that attempted to elicit information about the levels of respondents' economic satisfaction or dissatisfaction. As is apparent, the early Goldwater group has the smallest percentage of wholly unsatisfied members and almost the smallest percentage of highly satisfied respondents. Their modal response was "More or less satisfied," which seems somewhat surprising considering their relatively high level of income in absolute terms. Additionally, although the early Goldwater supporters are some- what less satisfied than most of the others, they are not by any means pessimistic about their economic future, as just less than half of them (49 percent) report that their economic situation has been getting better over the past few years (45.6 percent of the sample as a whole gave this response).

From these data we might infer that while no grave economic concerns seem to threaten any of the groups of respondents, there is some evidence of economic discontent among the wealthiest group. Perhaps this pattern of responses is the result of their relatively high tax rates, and these, coupled with their consistent opposition to federal expenditures for social welfare, make affirmation of complete economic satisfaction unlikely simply on ideological grounds.

Another index of economic stability is home ownership, and here again the early Goldwater group is considerably above the other groups. Eighty-two percent of these respondents owned their homes; 73.8 percent of the later supporters, 68.5 percent of the Johnson supporters, and 58.9 percent of the undecided voters also reported home ownership. Furthermore, the early Goldwater supporters were most likely to be living in more expensive neighborhoods than those they had lived in before moving to their current addresses. And it is also evident that Goldwater's supporters were generally more suburban in their residence pattern, with almost 45 percent of them reporting their last move as taking them farther from the center of the city than before. Finally,

TABLE III.4

Home Ownership of Candidate-Preference Groups, 1964

	Own		*Rent*		*Other*		*Total*	
	N	*%*	*N*	*%*	*N*	*%*	*N*	*%*
Early Goldwater supporters	82	82.0%	17	17.0%	1	1.0%	100	100.0%
Later Goldwater supporters	158	73.8	49	22.9	7	3.3	214	100.0
Johnson supporters	558	68.5	243	29.8	14	1.7	815	100.0
Undecided and other	224	58.9	143	37.6	13	3.4	380	100.0
Total	1,022	67.7	452	30.0	35	2.3	1,509	100.0

TABLE III.5

Cost of Homes of Candidate-Preference Groups
Compared to Cost of Former Homes, 1964

	Less		*Same*		*More*		*Total*	
	N	*%*	*N*	*%*	*N*	*%*	*N*	*%*
Early Goldwater supporters	51	51.0%	34	34.0%	15	15.0%	100	100.0%
Later Goldwater supporters	95	45.5	84	40.2	30	14.4	209	100.0
Johnson supporters	302	38.2	382	48.3	107	13.5	791	100.0
Undecided and other	143	38.8	177	48.0	49	13.3	369	100.0
Total	591	43.4	677	42.6	201	14.1	1,469	100.0

TABLE III.6

Location of Homes of Candidate-Preference Groups
Compared to Former Locations, 1964

	Closer to City Center		Same		Farther from City Center		Total	
	N	*%*	*N*	*%*	*N*	*%*	*N*	*%*
Early Goldwater supporters	24	23.8%	32	31.7%	45	44.6%	101	100.0%
Later Goldwater supporters	44	21.2	74	35.6	90	43.3	208	100.0
Johnson supporters	175	22.2	321	40.6	294	37.2	790	100.0
Undecided and other	101	27.5	146	39.8	120	32.7	367	100.0
Total	344	23.7	573	36.9	549	39.4	1,466	100.0

TABLE III.7

Age of Neighborhoods of Candidate-Preference Groups
Compared to Former Neighborhoods, 1964

	Newer		Same		Older		Total	
	N	*%*	*N*	*%*	*N*	*%*	*N*	*%*
Early Goldwater supporters	51	51.0%	34	34.0%	15	15.0%	100	100.0%
Later Goldwater supporters	95	45.4	84	40.2	30	14.4	209	100.0
Johnson supporters	302	38.2	382	48.3	107	13.5	791	100.0
Undecided and other	143	38.8	177	48.0	49	13.3	369	100.0
Total	591	43.4	677	42.6	201	14.1	1,469	100.0

they also were more likely to have moved into newer neighborhoods than the other respondents. Tables III.4 to III.7 report the data for all groups on home ownership, cost of homes, home location, and age of neighborhood.

Not only were Goldwater's early supporters disproportionately high in income level with respect to the population as a whole, but they were also an elite group among potential Republican voters. Since we would normally expect Republicans to have generally higher levels of income, education, and occupational status than either Democrats or undecided voters, this finding of high-status bias among *early* pro-

Goldwater Republicans is rather interesting. The division in the Republican voting bloc was the reverse of that suggested by White: the relatively elite segment of the Republican party's mass base disproportionately supported the primitives' candidate. Of course, the data presented here do not account for the probable shift of approximately 10 percent of normally loyal Republicans to the Johnson ticket, but in any case the rather high absolute level of social status of the early Goldwater group is still apparent; and while the effect of that shift may have been to remove persons of fairly high status from the group of later supporters of Senator Goldwater, it was not of sufficient size to obviate this finding.

Accompanying the high economic level of the early Goldwater supporters were, as I have indicated, the correlates of this favored condition: advanced levels of formal education and upper white-collar occupational roles. Accordingly, when we examine the self-reported social-class level of the various candidate-preference groups, the early supporters of Senator Goldwater are dominantly found to be middle class in their identification. Table III.8 shows the early Goldwater supporters to be 17.5 percentage points above the later Goldwater supporters and 34.6 percentage points above the Johnson supporters in this respect. Thus, as we would expect, the early Goldwater group and the Johnson supporters had distinctly different class orientations; although, of course, in absolute terms a greater number of middle-class respondents supported Johnson.

TABLE III.8

Self-Reported Social Class of
Candidate-Preference Groups, 1964

	Middle Class		*Working Class*		*Total**	
	N	*%*	*N*	*%*	*N*	*%*
Early Goldwater supporters	72	70.6%	23	22.5%	102	93.1%
Later Goldwater supporters	113	53.1	91	42.7	213	95.8
Johnson supporters	296	36.0	513	62.4	822	98.4
Undecided and other	126	33.4	242	64.2	377	97.6
Total	607	40.1	869	57.4	1,514	97.5

*Excluded from table, but computed in percentage base, are persons giving other answers to the question.

The intergenerational mobility of the three candidate-preference groups appears to have been about equal. Table III.9 details this generally consistent pattern. The early Goldwater group, however, experienced a small but relatively greater decline in the number of working-class respondents, a very slight indication of somewhat greater mobility on their part.

TABLE III.9

Intergenerational Mobility of Candidate-Preference Groups, 1964:
Respondents' and Families' Social-Class Identification
(In Percentages)

	Social-Class Identification		
	Respondents	*Respondents' Families*	*Net Change*
MIDDLE-CLASS RESPONDENTS			
Early Goldwater supporters	70.6%	62.5%	+8.1%
Later Goldwater supporters	53.1	44.5	+8.6
Johnson supporters	36.0	26.7	+9.3
Undecided and other	33.4	25.3	+8.1
Total	40.1	31.1	+9.0
WORKING-CLASS RESPONDENTS			
Early Goldwater supporters	22.5	37.5	−15.0
Later Goldwater supporters	42.7	53.6	−10.9
Johnson supporters	62.4	73.0	−10.6
Undecided and other	64.2	74.7	−10.5
Total	57.4	68.5	−11.1

Table III.10 reports a number of details concerning the region, population, sex, age, race, and marital status of the various groups.

Immediately evident is the fact that Goldwater's early support was drawn heavily from the South and border states (43.8 percent) and West (18.1 percent), with very little support from the Middle Atlantic and eastern states (7.7 percent). The later supporters, in contrast, were more evenly distributed among the various regions of the country, with 20.6 percent from the eastern and Middle Atlantic states, 34.7 percent from the Midwest, 29.2 percent from the southern and border states, and 15.6 percent from the West. These compare with the sample's distribution of 22.3 percent from the New England and Middle Atlantic states, 31.3 percent from the Midwest, 30.6 percent from the southern and border states, and 15.8 percent from the mountain and Pacific states.

Early Goldwater supporters differed from the other candidate-preference groups in the rather large proportion (about one-third) of them who lived in small towns. This tendency is also shared by the later Goldwater supporters. About 25 percent of them lived in small towns, whereas less than 20 percent of Johnson's backers resided in towns of this size. This is a pattern that is common to the distribution of Democratic and Republican party identification and voting; Republicans are usually found in smaller cities and towns. And this is, of course, also reflected in the heavy (14.5 percent) representation of Johnson's partisans in the twelve largest standard metropolitan statistical areas.

There was a heavy overrepresentation of males in the group of early Goldwater supporters. Fifty-seven percent of these respondents were males; only 44.7 percent of the later supporters and of the sample as a whole were male. This distribution is probably an artifact of the high levels of political activity among Goldwater's early supporters. As we know, males are much more active in politics than females.

The early Goldwater group was *less likely* to have older (sixty years or more) persons in it than the later Goldwater group, and more likely to have relatively young members. Between Johnson backers and all Goldwater supporters, however, there was a notable difference in the percentage of older supporters. Goldwater, with 21 percent of the electorate supporting him, had 31 percent of the persons sixty years and older behind him, whereas only 22 percent of Johnson's supporters were sixty and older.

As might have been expected on the basis of Goldwater's vote against the Civil Rights Act of 1964, there were no Negroes in our samples of either the early or later group of his supporters.

Goldwater's early backers were most likely to be married, another indication of their high economic stability, and the early and late groups of his backers were lowest in the number of divorced respondents. The

TABLE III.10

Demographic Characteristics of Candidate-Preference Groups, 1964

	Early Goldwater Supporters		Later Goldwater Supporters		Johnson Supporters		Undecided and Other		Total	
	N	%	N	%	N	%	N	%	N	%
REGION										
East and Middle Atlantic states	8	7.7%	45	20.6%	222	26.6%	70	18.1%	345	22.3%
Midwest	32	30.4	76	34.7	267	31.9	109	28.2	484	31.3
South and border states	46	43.8	64	29.2	210	25.1	154	39.8	474	30.6
Mountain and Pacific states	19	18.1	34	15.6	137	16.4	54	14.0	244	15.8
Total	105	100.0%	219	100.0%	836	100.0%	387	100.0%	1,547	100.0%
POPULATION*										
Metropolitan area†	10	9.5%	15	6.8%	121	14.5%	43	11.1%	189	12.2%
50,000 and over	18	17.1	41	18.7	162	19.4	85	22.0	306	19.8%
10,000–49,999	15	14.3	38	17.4	155	18.5	78	20.2	286	18.5
2,500– 9,999	33	31.4	56	25.6	151	18.1	74	19.1	314	20.3
Rural area	29	27.6	69	31.5	247	29.5	107	27.6	452	29.2
Total	105	100.0%	219	100.0%	836	100.0%	387	100.0%	1,547	100.0%
SEX										
Male	60	57.1%	98	44.7%	374	44.7%	159	41.1%	691	44.7%
Female	45	42.9	121	55.3	462	55.3	228	58.9	856	55.3
Total	105	100.0%	219	100.0%	836	100.0%	387	100.0%	1,547	100.0%

TABLE III.10 (Continued)

	Early Goldwater Supporters		Later Goldwater Supporters		Johnson Supporters		Undecided and Other		Total	
	N	%	N	%	N	%	N	%	N	%
AGE										
21–30	16	15.2%	21	9.6%	113	13.5%	72	18.6%	222	14.4%
31–39	18	17.1	37	16.9	175	20.9	63	16.3	293	18.9
40–49	24	22.9	52	23.7	184	22.0	70	18.1	330	21.3
50–59	21	20.0	40	18.3	179	21.4	73	18.9	313	20.2
60 and older	26	24.8	69	31.5	185	22.1	109	28.2	389	25.2
Total	105	100.0%	219	100.0%	836	100.0%	387	100.0%	1,547	100.0%
RACE										
White	105	100.0%	218	100.0%	721	86.5%	332	87.8%	1,376	93.5%
Negro	0	0.0	0	0.0	113	13.5	46	12.2	159	6.5
Total	105	100.0%	218	100.0%	834	100.0%	378	100.0%	1,535	100.0%
MARITAL STATUS										
Married	88	83.8%	156	71.2%	641	76.7%	290	74.9%	1,175	76.6%
Single	6	5.7	14	6.4	52	6.2	28	7.2	100	6.4
Divorced/separated	5	4.8	10	4.6	52	6.2	27	7.0	94	5.7
Widowed	6	5.7	39	17.8	91	10.9	42	10.9	178	11.3
Total	105	100.0%	219	100.0%	836	100.0%	387	100.0%	1,547	100.0%

*Standard size code for survey of consumer finances.

†Central cities of twelve largest standard metropolitan statistical areas.

TABLE III.11

Religion and Church Attendance of Candidate-Preference Groups, 1964

	Early Goldwater Supporters		Later Goldwater Supporters		Johnson Supporters		Undecided and Other		Total	
	N	%	N	%	N	%	N	%	N	%
RELIGION										
Catholic	20	19.0%	37	16.9%	227	27.2%	60	15.5%	344	22.3%
Orthodox	0	0.0	3	1.4	4	.5	0	0.0	7	.5
Jewish	1	1.0	0	0.0	38	4.5	6	1.6	45	2.9
General Protestant*	4	3.8	6	2.7	27	3.2	15	3.9	52	3.4
Reformation Protestant†	34	32.4	67	30.6	126	15.1	62	16.0	289	18.7
Pietistic Protestant‡	36	34.3	89	40.6	323	38.6	160	41.3	608	39.4
Neo-fundamentalist§	4	3.8	8	3.7	51	6.1	42	10.9	105	6.8
Nontraditional Christian¶	3	2.9	3	1.4	14	1.7	15	3.9	35	2.3
Other	3	2.9	6	2.7	22	2.6	27	7.0	58	3.8
Total	105	100.0%	219	100.0%	832	100.0%	387	100.0%	1,543	100.0%

TABLE III.11 (Continued)

	Early Goldwater Supporters		Later Goldwater Supporters		Johnson Supporters		Undecided and Other		Total	
	N	%	N	%	N	%	N	%	N	%
CHURCH ATTENDANCE										
Regular	52	51.5%	87	41.6%	368	46.3%	141	39.9%	648	44.5%
Often	20	19.8	37	17.7	136	17.1	62	17.6	255	17.5
Seldom	23	22.8	73	34.9	246	31.0	119	33.7	461	31.6
Never	6	5.9	12	5.7	44	5.5	31	8.8	93	6.4
Total	101	100.0%	209	100.0%	794	100.0%	353	100.0%	1,457	100.0%

*Persons responding only "Protestant."

†Presbyterian, Lutheran, Congregational, Evangelical Reformed, Dutch or Christian Reformed, United Church of Christ, Episcopalian, Anglican.

‡Methodist, African Methodist Episcopal, United or Evangelical Brethren, Baptist, Disciples of Christ, Christian.

§United Missionary, Church of God, Nazarene or Free Methodist, Church of God and Christ, Plymouth Brethren, Pentecostal or Assembly of God, Church of Christ, Salvation Army, Primitive Baptist, Free Will Baptist, Southern Baptist, Seventh-Day Adventist, other fundamentalists.

¶Christian Scientist, Spiritualist, Mormon, Unitarian, Jehovah's Witnesses, Quakers, Unity.

later group of supporters had a very high percentage (nearly 18 percent) of respondents who were widowed, a finding that we would expect in view of the relatively large number of older persons in this group.

The religious affiliation and frequency of church attendance of all the candidate-preference groups are given in Table III.11. Goldwater's early supporters have the highest percentage of Reformation Protestant members of any of the groups and the lowest proportion of pietistic Protestant members. There was almost no Jewish support for Goldwater at the pre- or postconvention level, and Catholics were much more likely, as is normally the case, to support the Democratic candidate (27.2 percent) than the Republican (17 percent). The proportions of the members of minority religious denominations and sects, including the neo-fundamentalists, nontraditional Christians, and non-Christians (excluding Jews), who supported Goldwater and Johnson are essentially equivalent. Among the undecided voters, however, these denominations had a much stronger foothold. Goldwater's early supporters were more often regular churchgoers than his later supporters, but they were not very different from Johnson's backers in their frequency of church attendance.

We have seen that Goldwater's early supporters were, relatively speaking, an elite segment of the population economically, and that they retained this position even within the total subset of potential Republican voters. They have been shown to have all the correlates of middle or upper middle social status and a high level of economic and social stability. They were predominantly Reformation Protestant in religious identification. Most of them lived in the southern and border states, with a slight overrepresentation in the West.

Thus the 1964 presidential election could be seen as a traditional contest between Republican and Democrat, as a southern-eastern conflict, as divided on more or less traditional class lines, or as the conflict of persons with great ideological differences. It is to these differences that we shall direct our attention in the following chapter.

CHAPTER IV

The 1964 Election:
Issues, Policy Preferences, and
the Scope of Political Extremism
Among Goldwater's Supporters

CIVIL RIGHTS, social welfare policy, and foreign affairs were, of course, the overt concerns of electoral politics in 1964. Underlying them, however, were two other highly salient issues that dominated the electorate's interpretation of the substantive issues of the campaign. These "meta-issues" were the widespread perception of Senator Goldwater as an irresponsible militarist and the common assertion that he and his supporters were political extremists and bigots.

CIVIL RIGHTS, PREJUDICE, AND THE
SUPPORTERS OF SENATOR GOLDWATER

If a single overt issue of domestic policy in 1964 could be said to have been the crux of the conflict among Republican political elites, it was the Civil Rights Act of that year. The conflict over the act and its implications for further extension of federal power into the area of civil rights for Negroes was followed by a series of riots in American cities in which the antagonists were police and Negroes. These issues, coupled with George Wallace's success in the Wisconsin and Indiana primary elections, lent an impressive facade to the supposed power of "white backlash." By the time of the Republican convention there had been a clear split among liberal and conservative Republicans over the civil rights issue, drawn primarily along the dimension of federal intervention on behalf of the civil rights movement. While the following paragraphs hardly form a comprehensive analysis of the racial and civil rights issues in 1964, they do at least suggest that there was distinct opposition among Goldwater's early supporters to federal intervention in the civil rights area and a fairly high level of approval of segregation and evidence of anti-Negro attitudes and policy preferences.

Table IV.1 presents the responses of the various groups to several questions dealing, first, with federal intervention in the civil rights area, and then with a series of questions that attempted to tap the electorate's feelings about segregation, the civil rights movement, and property rights.[1]

These data point to a fundamental division between Johnson and Goldwater supporters on the issue of federal intervention to establish equality of job opportunity and integrated schools. In each case, the response most hostile to such intervention was given by Goldwater's early supporters—in the case of school integration they were 22.5 percentage points above his later supporters in opposition to federal intervention and 34.1 points above Johnson's early backers. The difference between the early and later Goldwater supporters on the issue of federal intervention to ensure equality of job opportunity was small, but again a gulf separated all Goldwater supporters from those backing Johnson and, it is interesting to note, from the electorate as a whole.

The last three issues in this table were not related to the issue of federal power over traditionally local matters. Here the differences between Goldwater and Johnson supporters were in the same direction as they were on the first two issues, but by no means so extreme. Nor (with one or two exceptions) did the early or late backers of the senator deviate so strikingly from the entire electorate as they did on the civil rights–federal power issues. Nevertheless, it is clear that there was not only a strong reflection of the Republican elites' controversy over the issue of the role of the federal government in civil rights among Goldwater's supporters, but also a distinct tendency on their part to favor racial segregation, to oppose open occupancy, and to perceive the civil rights movement as more often violent than peaceful. Part of this probably may be explained by the heavy representation of southern and border-state respondents (43 percent of the total) in the early Goldwater group (see Table III.10); but the differences between the

[1]The intercorrelations between these two types of questions were low, but they were rather strongly associated within their category. The correlation between the first two items in the table was +.308; the mean correlation between these questions and the school integration items was +.133.

TABLE IV.1

Responses of Candidate-Preference Groups to Civil Rights Issues, 1964*

	Early Goldwater Supporters		Later Goldwater Supporters		Johnson Supporters		Undecided and Other		Total	
	N	%	N	%	N	%	N	%	N	%
EQUAL JOB OPPORTUNITY										
For government intervention	17	16.8%	43	20.5%	387	48.0%	160	50.3%	607	45.6%
Against government intervention	70	69.3	131	62.4	278	34.4	134	42.1	613	46.1
Total	87	86.1%	174	82.9%	665	82.4%	294	92.4%	1,220	91.7%
SCHOOL INTEGRATION										
For government intervention	24	23.1%	69	32.4%	402	49.8%	149	47.2%	644	47.8%
Against government intervention	69	66.3	113	43.8	266	32.9	140	44.3	588	43.8
Total	93	89.4%	182	76.2%	668	82.7%	289	91.5%	1,232	91.6%
SEGREGATION										
Favor	29	28.4%	58	27.5%	154	18.8%	104	27.9%	395	22.9%
Oppose	27	26.5	51	24.2	306	43.8	101	27.1	485	32.2
Total	56	54.9%	109	51.7%	460	62.6%	205	55.0%	830	55.1%
CIVIL RIGHTS MOVEMENT										
Seen as mostly violent	67	70.5%	149	75.6%	442	59.6%	220	57.9%	878	65.7%
Seen as mostly peaceful	22	23.2	43	21.8	265	35.7	89	33.4	419	28.5
Total	89	93.7%	192	97.4%	707	95.3%	309	91.3%	1,297	94.2%
OPEN OCCUPANCY										
Favor	48	45.7%	114	52.3%	519	62.4%	202	52.8%	883	53.3%
Oppose	38	36.2	63	28.9	190	22.8	109	28.5	400	29.1
Total	86	81.9%	177	81.2%	709	85.2%	311	81.3%	1,283	82.4%

*Percentages are computed only for those responding to the question. Responses reported exclude "no interest" and include "other" categories of response to each question as part of the percentage base. Total columns refer to percentage of respondents replying to the question in the manner indicated.

early and late groups of supporters are fairly small, and the later group had a slight underrepresentation of southerners on the basis of the distribution of the sample as a whole (see Table III.10). Both groups were entirely white. Obviously, then, the critics of Goldwater who identified his campaign and its supporters as generally opposed to equal opportunity for Negroes were in part correct; but Goldwater, on the other hand, correctly identified the overriding issue regarding civil rights as one of federal power and intervention in local and state affairs, not simply racism or segregation. In addition, when blacks are removed from these tabulations, the discrepancy between Goldwater and Johnson supporters is substantially diminished.

Clearly, the responses to the questions reported in Table IV.1 do not necessarily imply that the Goldwater groups were bigoted or prejudiced, any more than the seemingly more liberal responses of the Johnson supporters to the same questions mean that these respondents were integrationist, fair-minded contributors to the Southern Christian Leadership Conference. Part of the difference between Johnson and Goldwater supporters is simply a matter of adherence to their perceived parties' or candidates' positions on the issues raised by the questions. But it is rather surprising that groups with such extraordinarily high levels of formal education (see Table III.1) as the Goldwater supporters would favor segregation to the degree they did and so often oppose the right of a Negro to buy a house wherever he might choose to do so. Was prejudice a distinct characteristic of this group? There are some data that bear somewhat more directly on this point; let us examine them briefly.

Employing the feeling-thermometer technique described earlier, the Survey Research Center asked the respondents in the 1964 election studies to indicate the degree (on a scale of 100) of approval or disapproval of a number of ethnic groups and voluntary associations known to large segments of the mass public. As we have seen, this scale gives great flexibility to the measurement of the intensity and direction of an opinion, but it has been found to be a relatively unreliable indicator of attitudinal constraint except among persons with high levels of education; that is, a high rating of, say, liberals may be coupled with an equally high rating of conservatives. Among respondents with higher formal education, however, this tendency is attenuated, thus making the scale of some value for an analysis of the groups with which we are primarily concerned.

Besides blacks, two groups that have been traditional targets of prejudice are Jews and Catholics. The feeling-thermometer scores of the partisan segments on these two groups and on Negroes are reported

in Table IV.2. And as a preliminary glance at this table shows, there
appears to be a general pattern of antagonism toward Jews, Catholics,

TABLE IV.2

Candidate-Preference Groups' Evaluations of Jews, Catholics, and Negroes, 1964
(On Feeling-Thermometer Scale of 100°)

	Negative (<50°)		*Neutral* (50–59°)		*Positive* (>59°)		*Total*	
	N	*%*	*N*	*%*	*N*	*%*	*N*	*%*
EVALUATION OF JEWS								
Early Goldwater supporters	19	18.4%	27	26.2%	58	56.6%	104	100.0%
Later Goldwater supporters	18	8.5	82	38.5	113	53.1	213	100.0
Johnson supporters	67	8.2	307	37.4	447	54.4	821	100.0
Undecided and other	34	9.2	191	51.6	145	39.2	370	100.0
Total	138	9.2	607	40.3	763	50.6	1,508	100.0
EVALUATION OF CATHOLICS								
Early Goldwater supporters	13	12.5	25	24.0	66	63.5	104	100.0
Later Goldwater supporters	26	12.1	67	31.2	122	56.7	215	100.0
Johnson supporters	63	7.6	236	28.7	523	63.6	822	100.0
Undecided and other	40	10.8	152	41.2	177	48.0	369	100.0
Total	142	9.4	480	31.8	888	58.8	1,510	100.0
EVALUATION OF NEGROES								
Early Goldwater supporters	24	23.1	21	20.2	59	56.7	104	100.0
Later Goldwater supporters	36	16.7	52	24.2	127	59.1	215	100.0
Johnson supporters	97	11.9	211	25.8	510	62.3	818	100.0
Undecided and other	67	25.3	109	41.1	89	33.6	265	100.0
Total	224	16.0	393	28.0	785	56.0	1,402	100.0

and Negroes on the part of the early Goldwater supporters. They were twice as negative in their responses to Jews as the sample as a whole, slightly more hostile in their responses to Catholics, and about one and one-half times as negative in their views of Negroes as the entire sample. Of course, a small subset of this early Goldwater group was evidently responsible for this distribution of responses, because the early Goldwater supporters also provided a very high percentage of persons with positive attitudes toward these groups. Nevertheless, it is clear that there was a consistent and disproportionately high level of antagonism to these three minority groups by this subset of the early group which was not present in the responses of Goldwater's later supporters.

A natural assumption might be that these differences were produced by the relatively large number of southern respondents among

TABLE IV.3

Candidate-Preference Groups' Evaluations of Jews, by Region, 1964
(On Feeling-Thermometer Scale of 100°)

	Negative *(<50°)*		*Neutral* *(50–59°)*		*Positive* *(>59°)*		*Total*	
	N	*%*	*N*	*%*	*N*	*%*	*N*	*%*
SOUTH								
Early								
Goldwater								
supporters	8	17.4%	12	26.1%	26	56.5%	46	100.0%
Later								
Goldwater								
supporters	7	10.9	26	40.6	31	48.4	64	100.0
Johnson								
supporters	17	8.1	90	42.9	103	49.0	210	100.0
Undecided								
and other	13	8.1	88	55.0	59	36.9	160	100.0
Total	45	9.4	216	45.0	219	45.6	480	100.0
NONSOUTH								
Early								
Goldwater								
supporters	11	18.6	15	25.4	33	55.9	59	100.0
Later								
Goldwater								
supporters	13	8.4	56	36.1	86	55.5	155	100.0
Johnson								
supporters	52	8.2	215	33.8	369	58.0	636	100.0
Undecided								
and other	23	9.2	113	45.0	115	45.8	251	100.0
Total	99	9.0	399	36.3	603	54.8	1,101	100.0

the early Goldwater supporters. However, as a matter of fact, early southern supporters of the senator were *more likely* to hold *positive attitudes* toward Negroes and Jews than their northern counterparts, and were more favorably disposed toward Catholics and Jews than *any other* southern candidate-preference group. These findings are tempered somewhat by the fact that more hostility (scores of less than 50 degrees) toward Negroes and Jews (manifested in each case by only eight respondents) was also present among this group than among other later southern respondents.

TABLE IV.4

Candidate-Preference Groups' Evaluations of Catholics, by Region, 1964
(On Feeling-Thermometer Scale of 100°)

	Negative (<50°)		Neutral (50–59°)		Positive (>59°)		Total	
	N	%	N	%	N	%	N	%
SOUTH								
Early								
Goldwater								
supporters	5	10.9%	14	30.4%	27	58.7%	46	100.0%
Later								
Goldwater								
supporters	11	17.2	20	31.3	33	51.6	64	100.0
Johnson								
supporters	29	13.8	72	34.3	109	51.9	210	100.0
Undecided								
and other	19	11.9	81	50.6	60	37.5	160	100.0
Total	64	13.3	187	39.0	229	47.7	480	100.0
NONSOUTH								
Early								
Goldwater								
supporters	8	13.6	11	18.6	40	67.8	59	100.0
Later								
Goldwater								
supporters	15	9.7	47	30.3	93	60.0	155	100.0
Johnson								
supporters	34	5.4	164	26.2	428	68.4	626	100.0
Undecided								
and other	25	10.0	77	30.7	149	59.4	251	100.0
Total	82	7.5	299	27.4	710	65.1	1,091	100.0

Tables IV.3, IV.4, and IV.5 report these same data by place of residence. As an examination of the tables shows, the early Goldwater group in the South was consistently more liberal on this dimension of

TABLE IV.5

Candidate-Preference Groups' Evaluations of Negroes, by Region, 1964
(On Feeling-Thermometer Scale of 100°)

	Negative (<50°)		Neutral (50–59°)		Positive (>59°)		Total	
	N	%	N	%	N	%	N	%
SOUTH								
Early								
Goldwater								
supporters	8	17.4%	8	17.4%	30	65.2%	46	100.0%
Later								
Goldwater								
supporters	10	15.6	18	28.1	36	56.3	64	100.0
Johnson								
supporters	21	10.0	37	17.6	152	72.4	210	100.0
Undecided								
and other	20	12.5	46	28.8	94	58.8	160	100.0
Total	59	12.3	109	22.7	312	65.0	480	100.0
NONSOUTH								
Early								
Goldwater								
supporters	16	27.1	13	22.0	30	50.8	59	100.0
Later								
Goldwater								
supporters	27	17.3	34	21.8	95	60.9	155	100.0
Johnson								
supporters	77	12.3	175	28.0	374	59.7	626	100.0
Undecided								
and other	49	19.5	66	26.3	136	54.2	251	100.0
Total	169	15.5	288	26.3	635	58.2	1,091	100.0

attitude than the later supporters of the senator, and often more liberal than the backers of Lyndon Johnson.

Unexpectedly, but obviously, it was in the North that ethnic, racial, and religious hostility was strongest among Goldwater's early supporters; but even there (with the exception of Negroes) substantial majorities of his early backers were positively disposed to Jewish and Catholic minorities.

FOREIGN POLICY: MILITARISM, ANTICOMMUNISM, AND POLITICAL INVOLVEMENT

The issue of the questionable "responsibility" of Senator Goldwater was, as I indicated in the Preface, a very salient one for the American electorate in 1964. Angus Campbell summarizes the areas of the senator's image at which the electorate directed its criticisms:

It has been pointed out that Mr. Goldwater was much more commonly spoken of unfavorably than favorably. While he was more often referred to as a man of integrity than Mr. Johnson, and less commonly as a "politician," in most other respects he suffered from the comparison. He was especially weak in the public assessment of his past record and experience. His speeches drew much more criticism than Johnson's. His policy positions, as they were seen by the public, drew an exceptional number of comments, most of them unfavorable. While Mr. Goldwater obviously had many ardent admirers, the total public reaction to his personal qualities, his campaign appearances, and the policies with which he was identified was on balance clearly negative.[2]

And no single area drew so much criticism as did Goldwater's military policies—or what the electorate perceived to be his military policies. Of a total of 738 unfavorable references to Senator Goldwater's policy positions, 213 were directed at his militarism, 177 at his stand on social security, and only 81 at his opposition to civil rights. The remainder was distributed among his conservatism, his opposition to medicare, and his policies in general.[3] Very clearly, then, militarism and by extension foreign policy concerns were strikingly influential in the electorate's relatively negative evaluation of Senator Goldwater. This perception is even more remarkable when one looks at the data on the same issue from the 1960 election study. In 1960 the candidates were called too militaristic only twelve times in all, Nixon four times and Kennedy eight.[4]

There is a rather broad range of policy preferences and beliefs to which the larger issue of Goldwater's supposed militarism might be presumed to be related. Among these are, of course, overt concern about war in general and specifically the then relatively low-key conflict in Vietnam. But in addition such issues as foreign aid, the perceived position of the United States in world affairs, the strength of anti-communist feelings, and the respondent's views on negotiation and trade with communist nations all appear to tap concerns that, if not identical to a direct concern with militarism, at least are related to each other along the dimension of the respondent's preference for either a relatively conciliatory, flexible foreign policy or a rigid aggressive-isolationist

[2]Angus Campbell, "Interpreting the Presidential Victory," in *The National Election of 1964,* ed. Milton Cummings, Jr. (Washington, D.C.: Brookings Institution, 1966), pp. 256–81.
[3]*Ibid.,* pp. 261–62.
[4]*Ibid.,* p. 261.

posture on the part of his government.[5] There were a number of questions in the 1964 election study that explored these dimensions of opinion and attitude. Let us see to what extent the preferences and beliefs of Goldwater's supporters on these issues differed from or concurred with those of the other members of the electorate in 1964.

The responses of the candidate-preference groups to American involvement and policy in Vietnam presents an interesting, seemingly asymmetrical distribution of opinion on this question of foreign policy, which has, of course, become the central issue of American politics in the years ince these data were collected. (See Tables IV.6 and IV.7.)

TABLE IV.6

Opinions of Candidate-Preference Groups on Involvement in Vietnam, 1964

	Approve		Other		Disapprove		Total	
	N	%	N	%	N	%	N	%
Early Goldwater supporters	45	59.2%	1	1.3%	30	39.5%	76	100.0%
Later Goldwater supporters	74	51.7	4	2.8	65	45.5	143	100.0
Johnson supporters	329	66.1	5	1.0	164	32.9	498	100.0
Undecided and other	103	51.2	4	2.0	94	46.8	201	100.0
Total	551	60.0	14	1.5	353	38.5	918	100.0

While undecided voters were most likely to disapprove of Americans' involvement in Vietnam, they were closely followed by both groups of Goldwater's supporters, who were 6.6 and 12.6 percentage points, respectively, above the Johnson group's level of disapproval on this question. On the other hand, Goldwater's supporters differed markedly from the remainder of the electorate in the option they favored as a solution to America's presence in Vietnam: the early supporters of the senator favored escalation, including the invasion of North Vietnam, by a factor of almost two to one over Johnson's partisans and undecided voters. The later supporters of the senator were only slightly less aggressive in their choice of solutions.

It is somewhat ironic, given the immense growth of the conflict in Vietnam that occurred under Johnson's administration, that the majority

[5]These dimensions of policy preference seem to be the major ones to which the electorate as a whole responds. See Angus Campbell *et al., Elections and the Political Order* (New York: Wiley, 1966), pp. 355–56.

TABLE IV.7

Solutions to Vietnam Involvement Favored by Candidate-Preference Groups, 1964

	Pull Out		Retain Troops, Try to End Fighting		Take Stronger Stand, Including Invasion		Total	
	N	%	N	%	N	%	N	%
Early Goldwater supporters	9	11.2%	8	10.0%	63	78.9%	80	100.0%
Later Goldwater supporters	18	12.2	30	20.3	100	67.6	148	100.0
Johnson supporters	64	12.5	230	44.8	219	42.7	513	100.0
Undecided and other	34	18.3	84	45.2	68	36.6	186	100.0
Total	125	13.5	352	37.9	450	48.5	927	100.0

(57.3 percent) of his supporters in 1964 favored either a maintenance of the conflict at its 1964 level or pulling out of Vietnam entirely; and furthermore that the undecided voters also favored these alternatives even more strongly. Vietnam was the issue in 1964 around which the electorate's fear of militarism was organized, and although the electorate as a whole was almost evenly divided (48.6 percent for escalation, 51.4 percent against it) on this issue, the broad thrust of the Johnson vote was against escalation.

The militaristic segments of the electorate (with respect to the issue of Vietnam, anyway) were disproportionately found in the ranks of Goldwater's early backers. There was a difference of 11.3 percentage points between the early and late groups on this question, indicating that the voters who stayed with Goldwater, even though preferring another candidate, were likely to differ in a somewhat less militaristic direction from his earlier supporters on the issue of prosecuting the war in Vietnam. However, this difference is small when it is compared with Johnson's supporters and the sample as a whole. Since this group of later Goldwater supporters was made up largely of what might reason- ably be termed the party faithful (42 percent identified themselves as strong Republicans and an additional 38 percent said they were either not very strong or independent Republicans), the apparent militarism of Goldwater's campaign, while no doubt offending the defectors from the Republican ticket and independents and causing some concern among his later supporters, was probably not objectionable to the majority of Republicans in 1964. Evidently it would be a mistake to identify Goldwater's campaign as specifically responsible for the mobilization of militaristic sentiment among the electorate. It appears that a large majority of Republicans favored an aggressive policy in Vietnam and might well have done so regardless of who was heading the Republican ticket. As we shall see, despite the relative similarity in the two groups of Goldwater supporters along these two specific policy dimensions, they were widely divergent on another issue that might seem to be intimately related to the prosecution of a war against North Vietnam. This issue was anticommunism.

ANTICOMMUNISM

In 1964 the American electorate was generally in favor of negotiations with communist nations (84.3 percent favored this, only 11.4 percent opposed it), but on several other issues appeared to be unwilling to support policies that would increase U.S. involvement with communist states. For example, almost 57 percent of the electorate stated that "farmers and businessmen should be forbidden to do business with communist countries," and a large majority (74.9 percent) of those having an opinion on the issue opposed the admission of Red China to the United Nations. (Only 11.5 percent, however, felt that if Red China were admitted, the United States should withdraw from membership in the U.N.) The support of the electorate for American intervention to remove communist governments seems fairly strong: 39 percent favored doing "something to get the communist government out of Cuba," but almost half (48 percent) felt that it was "up to the Cuban people to handle their own affairs."

Aggressive, interventionist anticommunism was a strong theme of Goldwater's campaign, and, as we would expect, his early supporters were most likely to echo this theme in their responses to questions concerning American foreign policy. In order to measure the general level of anticommunist feeling among the electorate, an anticommunism index (ACI) was constructed by intercorrelating three items dealing with American policy toward communist nations; then, after establishing that there was a sufficiently close relationship among them for the purposes of an index (mean interitem correlation = + .422), each item was trichotomized into a three-point scale: 1 = low, 2 = medium, 3 = high; 0 was recorded for missing data. To determine scores, these index values were summed for the three items, and the range of possible scores (0–9) was again trichotomized, with a total score of 1, 2, or 3 becoming a 1 in the final scale, 4, 5, or 6 becoming 2, and 7, 8, or 9 becoming 3. The scores of the groups were then summed and expressed as percentages;[6] the distributions are reported in Table IV.8.

TABLE IV.8

Scores of Candidate-Preference Groups on Anticommunism Index (ACI), 1964

	Low		Medium		High		Total	
	N	%	N	%	N	%	N	%
Early Goldwater supporters	10	10.6%	33	35.1%	51	54.3%	94	100.0%
Later Goldwater supporters	40	21.4	87	46.5	60	32.1	187	100.0
Johnson supporters	267	38.5	330	47.6	96	13.9	693	100.0
Undecided and other	117	41.6	125	44.5	39	13.9	281	100.0
Total	434	34.6	575	45.8	246	19.6	1,255	100.0

A look at the high end of the distribution reveals extremely large differences among all groups with candidate preferences. Goldwater's early backers were more than 20 percentage points above his later supporters on this index, and Johnson supporters were slightly under 20 percentage points below the later Goldwater group.

Anticommunism by no means united all of Goldwater's eventual supporters in 1964, but it was one of the stronger discriminators between the blocs of Johnson and Goldwater supporters. But while the conception (evidenced by some critics) of the Republican party leader-ship and its supporters in 1964 as monolithically anticommunist is simply not borne out here, this is not to say that anticommunism as a political issue was unimportant in Republican politics at the mass level. Goldwater supporters, while at the time accounting for only about 21 percent of the electorate, contributed 45 percent of all the individuals scoring at the high end of the ACI. And inasmuch as the groups isolated here for analysis occupy a relatively elite political position, the extreme differences found here between Johnson and Goldwater sup-porters, like the similarly strong division between these groups on civil rights issues, suggest, as we would expect, that these issues are ideo-logically distinct for these groups in a very general sense. Intense anti-communism—a Goldwater campaign theme—was well received by the majority of his early supporters.

[6]This same procedure was used to develop all additional indices reported in this chapter. All items are reported in the Appendix.

Table IV.9 presents data about three additional areas of foreign policy on which some interesting differences are found among the groups. Like the ACI scores for the early Goldwater supporters, late Goldwater supporters, and Johnson supporters, the patterns of response on the issues of success in foreign relations and world position are widely divergent. Clearly, Goldwater's early supporters were extraordinarily agitated about these issues, and those who backed him soon after his nomination appear greatly disturbed about them as well. That dissatisfaction was so high among Goldwater's people may, of course, reflect simply their allegiance to the Republican party's position on foreign affairs, or it may reflect a genuine concern for the state of U.S. relations with other countries. If this is the case, these respondents might be expected to take something other than a traditional isolationist position on the question of foreign aid, and, as can be readily seen, they did.

As Table IV.9 indicates, both the early and late Goldwater backers supported foreign aid about half the time; two-thirds of Johnson's partisans backed it. But the spread between the early Goldwater group and the Johnson group is only 19 percentage points—a relatively small difference compared with ACI scores or the responses to the "foreign affairs" and "world position" questions. Thus, while a more traditional

TABLE IV.9

Candidate-Preference Groups' Perceptions of America's World Position and Views of Foreign Aid, 1964

	U.S. Not Doing as Well as It Should in Foreign Affairs		U.S. Position in the World Has Become Weaker		Favor Giving Aid to Foreign Countries That Need Help	
	N	%	N	%	N	%
Early Goldwater supporters	86	86.0%	61	61.0%	47	46.1%
Later Goldwater supporters	117	59.4	81	41.8	102	49.0
Johnson supporters	170	23.9	102	14.4	490	65.1
Undecided and other	105	40.5	78	25.2	180	54.1
Total	478	37.7	322	24.5	819	58.7

isolationism may be reflected in the tendency of Goldwater's supporters to object more often to foreign aid than their Democratic counterparts (and also in their opposition to America's initial involvement in Vietnam), a relative consensus on the issue is at least implied by these data, and its direction is clearly internationalist.

SOCIAL WELFARE

The issue of social welfare was, not surprisingly, fully as polarized as the issues of civil rights and foreign policy, and here too there was some discontinuity between the early and late Goldwater supporters. Goldwater's later supporters, for example, were 18 percentage points higher in approval of medicare, nearly 10 points higher in aid to employment, and 8.6 points higher in approval of aid to education than the early backers of the senator. But again these differences are relatively small when compared with the differences between the responses of Goldwater's supporters as a whole and those of either Johnson's backers or the undecided voters. Typically, spreads of 30 and 40 percentage points are found between the senator's supporters and the other groups. Table IV.10 reports responses to three important social welfare issues: medicare, aid to employment, and aid to education.

From these three areas of American national and foreign policy, it is evident that some unusually intense differences of opinion existed among the relatively politicized segments of the electorate in 1964. It is also evident, and certainly of greater interest, that the early and later pro-Goldwater groups were often significantly divided on these questions, the later group manifesting a distinctly more liberal bent in its preferences. This consistent discrepancy between the direction and intensity of the attitudes and opinions of these two groups, of course, only confirms our common-sense judgments and expectations.

The evidence suggests that Goldwater's candidacy resulted in a substantial shift of voters from the Republican to the Democratic parties;[7] and the data reported here show that the party faithful who stayed with Goldwater by no means responded to the themes of his campaign in a consistently supportive way. It appears very likely that Goldwater not only got all the support he could expect from ideologically conservative Republicans but also managed to attract a sizable segment of the electorate whose views were rather less conservative than this relatively pure and eager group of his supporters. These groups made up only 7 percent and 14 percent of the electorate respectively.

[7]Campbell, "Presidential Victory," pp. 279–81.

TABLE IV.10

Candidate-Preference Groups' Positions on Social Welfare Issues, 1964*

	Favor Medicare		Oppose Medicare		Favor Aid to Employment		Oppose Aid to Employment		Favor Aid to Schools		Oppose Aid to Schools	
	N	%	N	%	N	%	N	%	N	%	N	%
Early Goldwater supporters	13	13.4%	72	74.2%	8	8.2%	78	80.4%	12	12.2%	81	82.7%
Later Goldwater supporters	62	31.3	123	62.1	35	17.6	146	73.4	41	20.8	147	74.6
Johnson supporters	501	72.5	140	20.3	311	44.1	289	40.9	311	45.5	332	48.6
Undecided and other	189	62.4	94	31.0	127	40.4	152	48.4	122	42.2	150	51.9
Total	765	59.3	429	33.3	481	36.6	665	50.5	486	38.4	710	56.0

*Only the percentages of the candidate-preference groups responding as stated in the table are reported.

In their choice of Richard Nixon and rejection of Ronald Reagan in 1968, the Republican conservative elites evidently recognized that the nomination of a candidate whose views appeared to be as divergent as Goldwater's from those of even their loyal party members could not carry a national election. While there was a small segment of the electorate that mobilized itself around Goldwater's candidacy, the major thrust of its activities and of his campaign was to polarize the elite of the Republican party and to make more than obvious the fact that the levels of support for the policy positions favored by Goldwater and his followers were insignificant in comparison with the remainder of the American people, who felt, on the whole, very differently about the issues that faced them in the election of 1964.

THE CAMPAIGN OF 1964

If the level of political involvement in the 1964 Republican campaign seemed to many observers to be entirely out of proportion to the actual percentage of the electorate that supported the Republican candidate, it was because Goldwater's early supporters were by far the most active and involved segment of the electorate during 1964. They manifested a high sense of political efficacy and involvement. Even for persons of their rather advanced educational achievements, they possessed high levels of political information and high rates of exposure to the political process, the media, and the campaign.

For example, 70 percent of the early Goldwater group was at the high end of the Survey Research Center's index of political involvement, while only about 40 percent of both the Johnson supporters and the later Goldwater backers stood this high on the scale. As Converse, Clausen, and Miller point out,[8] the early Goldwater supporters were not only involved in the sense of being concerned about the outcome of the election and very much interested in the campaign; they were sufficiently active to send, in absolute numbers, more letters in support of their candidate to elites and the news media than any other segment of the electorate. And there is every reason to believe that this pre-convention activity was carried over with redoubled effort into the campaign itself. Converse and his colleagues suggest that a portion of the rational basis of the Goldwater campaign (that is, the premise that Goldwater could win) may have rested upon this high level of activity on the part of Goldwater's early supporters and in particular on the

[8]Philip E. Converse, Aage R. Clausen, and Warren E. Miller, "Electoral Myth and Reality: The 1964 Election," *American Political Science Review*, 59, no. 2 (June 1965): 321–36.

high media visibility that their preferences presumably commanded by reason of their high rate of political letter-writing.

But visibility in the national media was not the only probable reason for the misjudgment of support for Goldwater by Republican conservative elites. Goldwater, while very much a minority candidate, was able to field a greater number of involved and active supporters than was Johnson. Surely at least part of the judgment that Goldwater could win was influenced by the presence of this field of dedicated supporters. Certainly it must have seemed to many Republican elites that a Goldwater boom was not simply in the making but was already

TABLE IV.11

Levels of Political Activity as Measured by Political Activity Index (PAI), Controlled for High and Low Levels of Political Involvement, 1964*

	Low Activity		Medium Activity		High Activity		Total	
	N	*%*	*N*	*%*	*N*	*%*	*N*	*%*
HIGH POLITICAL INVOLVEMENT								
Early Goldwater supporters	0	0.0%	35	50.7%	34	49.3%	69	100.0%
Later Goldwater supporters	0	0.0	50	62.5	30	37.5	80	100.0
Johnson supporters	2	0.7	231	79.4	58	19.9	291	100.0
Undecided and other	0	0.0	48	77.4	14	22.6	62	100.0
Total	2	0.4	364	72.5	136	27.1	502	100.0
LOW POLITICAL INVOLVEMENT								
Early Goldwater supporters	1	3.6	17	60.7	10	35.7	28	100.0
Later Goldwater supporters	11	8.9	99	80.5	13	10.6	123	100.0
Johnson supporters	41	8.2	434	87.1	23	4.6	498	100.0
Undecided and other	61	20.5	229	77.1	7	2.4	297	100.0
Total	114	12.1	779	82.3	53	5.6	946	100.0

*Respondents dichotomized on the basis of high and low scores on the SRC index of political involvement. Items listed in Appendix.

a fact of American political life in the summer and fall of 1964. And while we have seen that there was a fatal discrepancy between the general ideological orientation of Goldwater's early supporters and much of the remainder of the electorate, the scope of this discrepancy, if it was visible to the conservative Republican elites, was no doubt balanced in their minds by what they also knew to be true: many extraordinarily dedicated people supported Goldwater. Perhaps that was all he needed to win.

A simple measure of political activism was constructed in the same fashion as the ACI, with seven items dealing with opinion leadership, attendance at political meetings, working for a party or candidate, and the like. Table IV.11 presents the distribution of the various groups on this index, controlled for high and low levels of political involvement.

The early supporters of Senator Goldwater were clearly much more likely than the other groups to have accompanied their involvement (i.e., interest in and concern about outcome) in the campaign by actual political activity. Even when involvement with the campaign was low, this group was extraordinarily active in politics. Among those with high political involvement, of course, the differences between Goldwater's late and early supporters may simply be artifacts of their own preferences prior to the convention, with early Goldwater partisans simply backing their man more strongly during the campaign, as would be expected in any factional situation. Yet while this effect may be present to some degree, the later supporters of the senator were still, regardless of the degree of their involvement in the campaign, much higher on the PAI than any other group except the initial backers of the Republican nominee.

While these findings are very much in line with what we know about Republicans and persons of high socioeconomic status as participants in the political arena—namely, that they are usually more active as a group than Democrats—it is interesting to note the much greater consistency between high involvement and high activism among the early Goldwater group than among all others. As we have seen, 70 percent of this group scored at the high end of the involvement index and half of this subset fell at the high-activity end of the PAI. Only 39 percent of the later Goldwater group manifested the same degree of involvement and of these only a little more than a third scored at the high end of the PAI. Only 40 percent of Johnson supporters were at the high-involvement end of the SRC index, and of these only about a fifth demonstrated high levels of political activism.[9] Goldwater was able

---

[9]When these groups are controlled for level of political involvement, the differences between them become even more extreme.

TABLE IV.12

Strength of Party Identification of Candidate-Preference Groups, 1964

	Strong Democrat		Not Very Strong Democrat		Independent Democrat		Independent		Independent Republican		Not Very Strong Republican		Strong Republican		Total	
	N	%	N	%	N	%	N	%	N	%	N	%	N	%	N	%
Early Goldwater supporters	6	5.8%	13	12.5%	2	1.9%	7	6.7%	23	22.1%	15	14.4%	38	36.5%	104	100.0%
Later Goldwater supporters	9	4.1	21	9.7	4	1.8	10	4.6	17	7.8	65	30.0	91	41.9	217	100.0
Johnson supporters	350	42.0	245	29.4	93	11.2	38	4.6	17	2.0	72	8.6	19	2.3	834	100.0
Undecided and other	51	14.2	103	28.8	43	12.0	58	16.2	30	8.4	51	14.2	22	6.1	358	100.0
Total	416	27.5	382	25.2	142	9.4	113	7.5	87	5.8	203	13.4	170	11.2	1,513	100.0

to muster supporters whose consistent dedication to his cause was without parallel among the electorate in 1964. It was a mustering based in part, of course, on the high SES levels of his backers, but it was also enlarged by unusual levels of dedication.

Unfortunately, from his point of view, these dedicated persons made up only about 4 percent of the electorate, even though they accounted for almost 40 percent of the high-activity–high-involvement subset of the public and more than 50 percent of the active-involved group with a candidate preference. Thus the Goldwater strategists were correct in proposing the theory of the existence of a hard core of conservatives willing to give almost everything for the election of a conservative Republican candidate. Many persons did support Goldwater with a degree of faithfulness and dedication that certainly appears to be extraordinarily high. But of course they were mistaken in believing that there were enough of them to carry the election. That Goldwater did as well as he did on November 3 may very well be attributed to the fact that during the campaign he had more politically active and involved supporters than the winner of the election, Lyndon B. Johnson.

PARTISAN CHOICE

Earlier in this chapter some mention was made of the partisan makeup of the early Goldwater supporters and of the rates of infusion and defection from partisan ranks in the 1964 election. Table IV.12 provides some data about the party identification of Goldwater's supporters and of the probable net shifts between the parties in 1964. What is immediately evident from these data is that, although heavily Republican in their party identification, Goldwater's early backers were more likely than his postconvention supporters to identify themselves as independent Republicans or as Democrats. Seemingly the early Goldwater group was composed of persons with an unusually high degree of independence from political party structure. These findings also seem to reinforce the contention of the conservative Republican elites that either (*a*) persons alienated from (i.e., independent of) the Republican party would support Goldwater more strongly than anyone else now that the party had at last supplied them with an acceptable candidate—which in fact seems to have been the case—or (*b*) a coalition of conservatives would form, irrespective of party identification, and back Senator Goldwater for the presidency. Both these things evidently occurred, but of course the number of such persons was insufficient to effect a victory.

How much the Republicans lost and how much the Democrats

gained from the short-term influence of Goldwater's candidacy is an extremely complicated question,[10] and the answer that is suggested here is by no means definitive—first and foremost because this is not an analysis of voting as such. But some idea of the effects of his candidacy on the more politically involved segment of the electorate may be gained from brief consideration of the data in Table IV.12. Of all Johnson supporters, 12.9 percent identified themselves as Republicans of some type, the majority of them saying that they were "not very strong" Republicans. This amounts to about 11 percent of the subset of the sample with a partisan choice shifting to the Democratic ticket. Among the supporters of Goldwater (early and late), 17.9 percent volunteered a Democratic identification, or about 4 percent of the same partisan-choice subset. Proportionally speaking, then, Goldwater got slightly more Democratic support than he lost from Republicans; but in absolute terms, of course, his net loss to the Democrats was almost three times the gains he made by attracting conservative or dissident Democrats to his candidacy. And as Campbell has shown, the overall percentage of votes gained by the Democratic party in 1964 was several percentage points greater than could be accounted for by either sampling error or the normal net variation in the vote of something less than 6 percent.[11] Goldwater's nomination resulted in some sharp turnover among persons with high and moderately high levels of party identification; and if this new pattern of identification is retained in these strata of the electorate, it suggests that a first step in the realignment of American parties may be occurring. As the other data we have considered indicate, the direction of this realignment is toward a greater polarization along the well-worn but in this case useful dimension of liberalism and conservatism.[12]

THE POLITICAL SOCIALIZATION OF GOLDWATER'S SUPPORTERS: DEMOCRATIC INSTITUTIONS AND THE QUESTION OF EXTREMISM

In addition to the questions of the strength and nature of the partisan identification of the various groups that we have examined, there is another interesting issue, raised loudly during the 1964 campaign, concerning the extent to which Goldwater's supporters were or were not socialized political actors. That is, to what degree did they overtly support and practice American-style democratic politics? Or

[10]See Campbell, "Presidential Victory," pp. 279–81.
[11]*Ibid.*
[12]*Ibid.*

were they, as charged by Richard Rovere, simply a group of infil-
trators?[13] Part of this question resulted from the extraordinarily high
percentage of new (and pro-Goldwater) delegates to the Republican
National Convention, leading Aaron Wildavsky, in his discussion of
the ideological predispositions of these delegates, to conclude that a
new class of persons, lacking a realistic approach (or, as he says, taking
a purist approach) to part politics, was now in a position to exert
strong influence on the Republican party.[14] Costantini and Craik, in a
paper dealing with the political and psychological characteristics of the
two competing California delegations (Goldwater and Rockefeller) to
the convention, found, however, that the Goldwater delegation, from
California at least, was new neither to politics nor to the Republican
party. In fact, the Goldwater delegates' commitment to their party, as
reflected in their holding of county and state offices, the length of their
participation in party affairs, the proportion of their incomes contributed to the party, and their attendance at national party conventions,
was in every case greater and often twice as great as that of the
Rockerfeller delegates.[15] In part, of course, these findings are unique
because of the nature of California's unusually polarized party system.
But they nevertheless point out that at the elite level the Goldwater
backers do not necessarily seem to have been either "seditious insur-
gents" or antiparty grass-roots anarchists. These data do reinforce
Wildavsky's point concerning ideological purity, however. As we have
seen at the mass level, the early backers of Goldwater expressed a
relatively independent party identification and had a lower rate of party
consistency in their voting history (45.2 percent stated they voted for
"different parties" vs. 34 percent of later supporters and 34.4 percent
of Johnson's supporters). But at the same time, the high PAI scores
of these early Goldwater supporters argue for a rather high level of
political socialization on their part.

A somewhat tangential approach to the question of the Goldwater
backers' political responsibility can be taken by looking at several sets
of variables. One of these concerns the degree of legitimacy that the
various groups of respondents assigned to American political institutions
such as elections, the Congress, and political parties. Presumably per-

[13]Richard Rovere, "American Letter," *Encounter,* 23 (October 1964), cited in
Edmond Costantini and Kenneth Craik, "Two Faces of Republican Leadership:
Goldwater and Rockefeller Elites in California," mimeographed (Berkeley:
Institute of Governmental Affairs, University of California, 1967), p. 49.

[14]Aaron Wildavsky, "The Goldwater Phenomenon: Purists, Politicians, and the
Two-Party System," *Review of Politics,* 27, no. 3 (July 1965): 386–413.

[15]Costantini and Craik, "Two Faces."

sons who see little effectiveness in these institutions—that is, think of them as being unrepresentative and unresponsive to the will of the people—also are likely to harbor doubts about their value. Of course, it is the nature of an opposition party to question the decisions of such institutions when they are controlled by the opposing party. Nevertheless, rejection of these institutions, if common among Goldwater's early supporters, might be taken as very tenuous confirmation of the argument put forth by Rovere and others that Goldwater's backers lacked a commitment to the democratic political order. Secondly, if Goldwater's supporters approved of extremist political organizations, such as the Ku Klux Klan and the John Birch Society, as they were so widely said to do, we might argue that supporting organizations like these is inconsistent with support for democratic norms. If some evidence could be found that Goldwater's partisans were backward-looking political dreamers rejecting the present in favor of a presumably idyllic past, it could be argued that this view of political life was essentially unrealistic and dysfunctional. Finally, if his early supporters were dogmatic and inflexible in their approach to life, might they not also be dogmatic and inflexible in their political actions, thus violating democratic norms of compromise and respect for the opposition's point of view? The remainder of this chapter will attempt to examine and perhaps answer these questions.

Let us look first at the electorate's perceptions of the legitimacy of the government and of American political institutions. A five-item series of questions in the postelection survey dealing with "different ideas people have about the government in Washington" was combined in an index labeled the Legitimacy of Government Index (LGI). The distribution of scores on this index is reported in Table IV.13. The modal score on the LGI is the midpoint. Very few respondents were willing to describe the government in perfectly rosy terms. Dissatisfaction was much more common, however, among Goldwater's early backers than among the other groups. While this finding in itself is of somewhat dubious meaning, since it is a more or less standard opposition response, it is paralleled by a similar pattern of responses to several questions concerning American political institutions. These responses were not reduced to an index, but are presented individually in Table IV.14. In every case, the early supporters of Senator Goldwater gave a small but greater proportion of responses questioning the effectiveness of the three agencies of representation (Congress, parties, and elections) than the other candidate-preference groups, and were 13 percentage points above the senator's later supporters in their overall belief in the unrepresentativeness of the government. These responses

TABLE IV.13

Scores of Candidate-Preference Groups on
Legitimacy of Government Index (LGI), 1964

	*LGI Scores**							
	Low		*Medium*		*High*		*Total*	
	N	*%*	*N*	*%*	*N*	*%*	*N*	*%*
Early Goldwater supporters	58	59.8%	38	39.2%	1	1.0%	97	100.0%
Later Goldwater supporters	99	48.8	95	46.8	9	44.4	203	100.0
Johnson supporters	205	26.0	557	70.7	26	3.3	788	100.0
Undecided and other	115	32.5	219	61.9	20	5.6	354	100.0
Total	477	33.1	909	63.0	56	3.9	1,442	100.0

*See Appendix for index items.

do not seem too surprising considering the divergence of their opinions
from then current government policy.

Although I do not believe that any but the most tentative conclusions may be drawn from these two patterns of responses, it does
seem reasonable to conclude that the early Goldwater group did manifest a lack of faith in democratic processes. They were, in fact, more
often willing to give pessimistic and disaffected responses to questions
concerning American political institutions and government than most of
the mass public. In any case, the evidence does not support any particular interpretation very strongly, and there is certainly no strong support
here for an identification of Goldwater's followers as generally alienated
or hostile to the democratic institutions of American political life.

A finding of some theoretical importance, however, appears when
one compares the responses of the early Goldwater supporters to the
questions on the Legitimacy of Government Index with the high sense
of political efficacy exhibited by this group. These data show that early
supporters of the senator were highly involved in politics and manifested
a high degree of efficacy while at the same time exhibiting relatively
large amounts of distrust.

These findings are not unique to Goldwater's backers. Indeed,
these attributes were common among the ghetto rioters in Newark and

TABLE IV.14

Agreement of Candidate-Preference Groups with Statements Questioning Legitimacy of Political Institutions, 1964*

	Government does not pay much attention to what the people think when it decides what to do		Political parties do not help much to make the government responsive to the people		Elections do not help much to make the government responsive		Congressmen do not pay much attention to their constituents when making decisions	
	N	%	N	%	N	%	N	%
Early Goldwater supporters	42	43.7%	18	19.1%	10	10.3%	20	20.8%
Later Goldwater supporters	60	30.6	33	17.4	20	10.2	35	17.8
Johnson supporters	146	19.7	79	10.7	28	3.7	102	13.6
Undecided and other	90	29.0	50	16.6	32	10.2	60	19.6
Total	338	25.2	180	13.6	90	6.6	217	16.1

*Only the percentages of the candidate-preference groups responding as stated in the table are reported.

Detroit studied by Paige[16] and student strikers I interviewed at San Francisco State College during the winter of 1968–1969. William A. Gamson, in a theoretical discussion of the preferred means of influence, political trust, and social control, has pointed to the importance of trust and efficacy in determining an interest group's mode of attempting to influence authorities. Low trust and high efficacy, he argues, produce attempts at coercive influence by the group in question.[17] It therefore seems appropriate to point out here that the low trust and high efficacy of Goldwater's supporters were linked in 1964 to a very intense, sometimes coercive, and ultimately successful attempt at influence on their part: the control of the presidential nomination of the Republican party.

TABLE IV.15

Support for Three Extremist Organizations, 1964:
John Birch Society, Christian Anti-Communism Crusade,
and Ku Klux Klan
(Scores >60° on Feeling Thermometer)

	John Birch Society		Christian Anti-Communism Crusade		Ku Klux Klan	
	N	%	N	%	N	%
Early Goldwater supporters	43	47.3%	16	41.0%	4	4.2%
Later Goldwater supporters	35	19.9	19	31.1	12	6.0
Johnson supporters	36	5.8	56	28.7	24	3.2
Undecided and other	13	5.4	13	18.8	11	3.5
Total	127	11.3	104	28.6	51	3.0

*Only the percentages of the candidate-preference groups responding as stated in the table are reported.

[16]Jeffery M. Paige, "Collective Violence and the Culture of Subordination: A Study of Participants in the July 1967 Riots in Newark, New Jersey, and Detroit, Michigan" (unpublished Ph.D. dissertation, University of Michigan, 1968).

[17]James McEvoy and Abraham Miller, "On Strike, Shut It Down: The Crisis at San Francisco State College," *Trans-action,* March 1969, pp. 18–23, 61–62; William A. Gamson, *Power and Discontent* (Homewood, Ill.: Dorsey Press, 1968), pp. 39–58, 163–84.

Another issue, raised during both the 1964 Republican convention and the ensuing campaign, was extremism or, more specifically, the supposed extremist support for Goldwater and his apparent reciprocal encouragement of extremist groups. The most prominent of these was the John Birch Society, an organization with which Goldwater had cooperated while a senator,[18] although he later became critical of its founder, Robert Welch. The measure of support for this organization employed in the SRC survey was the "feeling thermometer" discussed earlier, and the scoring of the John Birch Society by the various groups is reported in Table IV.15, along with their scores on the Christian Anti-Communism Crusade and the Ku Klux Klan, two other organizations often described as extremist.

As this table clearly demonstrates, the two groups of Goldwater's supporters were much more likely than Johnson's backers or the undecided voters to evaluate the John Birch Society and the Christian Anti-Communism Crusade favorably; and the early Goldwater supporters were particularly strong in their support of these organizations. This being the case, it may seem appropriate to answer our original question in the affirmative—that is, to accept the notion that Goldwater's early supporters were extremists. If we equate support for these groups with radical or extremist political values, there is no question that the early Goldwater supporters were disproportionately extremist. But, as we have seen, this high level of approval of the Birch Society and the Christian Anti-Communism Crusade was not accompanied by any wholesale rejection of democratic political institutions. This is not to say, however, that the three sets of findings presented here do not give support to the Rovere thesis; they do. But with the exception of the data on the extremist groups, this support is not terribly strong.

The last measures that bear on this point and with which we will close this discussion are two attempts to measure the degree of personal dogmatism and of yearning for the past among the respondents—two sets of concepts that have frequently been associated with the psychological components of conservatism. The first of these, personal dogmatism, was tapped by the three items reported in Table IV.16, concerning the respondent's ability to change his mind, his success in winning arguments, and the strength of his opinions. As can be seen, some interesting differences do emerge between the early Goldwater

[18]Specifically, by signing, with Robert Welch and a number of members of the council of the John Birch Society, an advertisement urging President Eisenhower to cancel a then impending visit to the United States by the former Russian premier Nikita Khrushchev. This advertisement was reprinted in *The Blue Book of the John Birch Society.*

supporters and the remainder of the electorate on the items having to do with strength of opinion and mental flexibility. Goldwater's early backers are about 30 percentage points above all of the other groups of respondents in the self-reported strength of their opinions and about 15 points higher than the others in their reported resistance to changing their minds. A certain mental rigidity definitely appears to characterize this group vis-à-vis all other groups isolated here for analysis.

TABLE IV.16

Self-Reported Personal Dogmatism of Candidate-Preference Groups, 1964*

	Always Gets Own Way in Arguments		Has Strong Opinions		Hard to Change Mind	
	N	%	N	%	N	%
Early Goldwater supporters	22	23.9%	72	74.2%	81	84.4%
Later Goldwater supporters	43	21.9	94	46.5	145	72.5
Johnson supporters	197	25.5	347	44.5	546	69.5
Undecided and other	66	19.6	123	43.9	232	67.8
Total	328	23.4	636	44.9	1,004	70.5

*Only the percentages of the candidate-preference groups responding as stated in the table are reported.

Somewhat surprising, however, are the data reported in Table IV.17. Contrary to much popular wisdom, there was no universal identification of the past as personally or morally idyllic on the part of Goldwater's early or later supporters. Nevertheless, there was a distinct tendency, reflected in the gap of 10 to 15 percentage points between all Goldwater's supporters and Johnson's backers on the first two items in the table, for the past to be viewed in a more sanguine fashion by the pro-Goldwater group. Despite the early Goldwater supporters' generally more negative evaluation of the trends of contemporary American political life, however, they did not differ very much from the senator's later supporters on these dimensions of opinion.

TABLE IV.17

Agreement of Candidate-Preference Groups with Statements
Reflecting Nostalgia for Past, 1964*

	Life Was Better 50 Years Ago		Life Was More Satisfying 50 Years Ago		It's Harder to Lead a Good Moral Life Now	
	N	%	N	%	N	%
Early						
Goldwater supporters	25	26.3%	44	47.3%	62	69.7%
Later						
Goldwater supporters	47	23.7	84	43.5	142	74.7
Johnson supporters	120	15.7	233	30.9	517	69.1
Undecided and other	77	23.3	119	36.4	234	73.4
Total	269	19.4	480	35.1	955	71.0

*Only the percentages of the candidate-preference groups responding as stated in the table are reported.

CONCLUSION

The theoretically interesting issues that may be investigated by the data presented here may conveniently be divided into the six general issue areas of political and social alienation, status discrepancy and status anxiety, populism and provincialism, religious fundamentalism, orientation toward major economic institutions, and partisan choice. As we shall see, some of these categories are also applicable to the Wallace movement.

With the cautionary note that it is a somewhat questionable enterprise to equate Goldwater's early supporters with right-wing extremists, a review of theoretical speculation about the origins of right-wing extremist groups may nevertheless be pertinent here, if only because of the fact that Goldwater's supporters were so often identified as extremists by the press and by the public.

A number of writers have proposed that right-wing extremists are "alienated." That is, they have suffered economic dislocation or some serious breakdown in primary-group associations, lack secondary-group memberships, and are detached from politics and political institutions. We may say quite firmly that these statements do not generally apply to the early supporters of Senator Goldwater. In fact, the opposite is the case. The early Goldwater supporters were highest in the proportion of members who are married and second lowest (to the later Goldwater supporters) in the proportion of divorced or separated members. They were also the most frequent churchgoers in the population. Almost 62 percent of the early Goldwater group had at least some college education and nearly 40 percent had incomes of $10,000 a year or more (see Table III.10). As we also know, their economic condition, as measured by such variables as home ownership and the comparative costs of the neighborhoods in which they had lived, seemed largely secure and comfortable (see Tables III.4–III.7). But of course it is still true that the early supporters of Senator Goldwater were slightly less content (see Table III.3) with their economic lot than were the other candidate-preference groups. Nevertheless, their minor discontent in the face of relative affluence hardly argues for economic alienation among this group. We have seen their very high level of participation in politics and their extraordinary sense of political efficacy and involvement. These are conditions that argue rather strongly against alienation —at least as the term is usually defined.

Although it was mentioned briefly earlier, the issue of status discrepancy (the presence of an imbalance in one or more components of socioeconomic status, such as very low income with very high education) deserves a more detailed examination. As I just noted, high income and educational attainment marked Goldwater's early supporters. The same was true of their occupational roles. They had the highest proportion of white-collar workers (by almost 20 percentage points) and the lowest proportion of blue-collar workers. An especially high percentage of them (28 percent) were self-employed businessmen, artisans, and managers, a finding that parallels that of Martin Trow in his important study of small businessmen's support for McCarthy in Bennington, Vermont.[19] As we shall see, however, Goldwater's supporters, while disproportionately sharing the economic roles Trow found to be associated with support for McCarthy, had quite a different orientation toward the major economic institutions of American society.

In their social-class identifications, the early Goldwater backers were overwhelmingly middle class (70.6 percent), 17.5 percentage points above their nearest rivals, postconvention Goldwater supporters. It does not appear, then, that there was very much status discrepancy among Goldwater's early supporters as a group. Furthermore, upward

[19]Martin Trow, "Right-Wing Radicalism and Political Intolerance: A Study of Support for McCarthyism in a New England Town" (unpublished Ph.D. dissertation, Columbia University, 1957), pp. 31–49.

TABLE IV.18

Status Discrepancy as Shown by Comparison of Occupation, Income, and Educational Attainment Among Candidate-Preference Groups, 1964*

	Grade School Education and Income > $10,000		Grade School Education and Upper White-Collar Occupation		At Least Some College and Income < $6,000		At Least Some College and Blue-Collar Occupation		Blue-Collar Occupation and Income > $10,000		Upper White-Collar Occupation and Income < $6,000	
	N	%	N	%	N	%	N	%	N	%	N	%
Early Goldwater supporters	3	2.9%	7	7.1%	11	10.6%	8	8.1%	3	3.1%	7	7.1%
Later Goldwater supporters	7	3.3	7	3.4	28	13.3	16	7.8	15	7.5	13	6.6
Johnson supporters	44	5.5	44	5.6	86	10.7	74	9.4	42	5.5	40	5.2
Undecided and other	12	3.3	23	9.7	27	7.3	21	8.9	13	5.7	20	8.7
Total	66	3.8	81	6.5	152	10.5	119	8.6	73	5.5	80	6.9

*Numbers and percentages refer to the proportion of each candidate-preference group matching the given condition of discrepancy.

intergenerational mobility appears to have been no greater among the early Goldwater supporters than among the later group or the Johnson supporters. Each group reports a gain of about 8 percent in middle-class status over the reported status of their parents (see Table III.9).

Additionally, in a series of cross-tabulations among the variables of occupations, income, and education *within* the various groups, no important differences were found between the early Goldwater supporters and the other groups in the proportion of members who were status discrepant. As Table IV.18 indicates, the proportion of each of the candidate-preference groups that manifested any of the discrepant conditions was rather small (a maximum of about 13 percent). And there is no consistent pattern of upward or downward discrepancy found here, either. In other words, the three discrepant conditions that imply upward social movement (a grade school education paired with an income of $10,000 or more, a grade school education and an upper white-collar occupation, and a blue-collar occupation with an income of $10,000 or more) are distributed about equally among the candidate-preference groups, as are the three discrepant conditions implying downward social mobility.

Finally, Table IV.19 reports the proportions of respondents in the various groups whose reported social-class memberships and educational levels are mismatched. When a person with a low (grade school) level of education reports a middle-class identification, we might suspect him to be suffering from *status anxiety,* a psychological variant of status discrepancy; presumably anxiety manifested about one's status, irrespective of its actual consistency, is a good predictor of right-wing

TABLE IV.19

Status Anxiety as Shown by Comparison of Candidate-Preference Groups'
Self-Reported Social Status with Level of Formal Education, 1964

	Middle Class Identification, Grade School Education		*Working Class Identification, at Least Some College*	
	N	*%*	*N*	*%*
Early Goldwater supporters	9	9.9%	6	6.6%
Later Goldwater supporters	23	11.3	22	10.8
Johnson supporters	70	8.7	106	13.1
Undecided and other	36	9.9	23	6.3
Total	138	10.0	157	9.2

Numbers and percentages refer to the proportion of each candidate-preference group matching the given condition of discrepancy.

extremism. As I noted in Chapter II, this idea has usually been measured by questions concerning the respondent's acceptance in his local community. While Table IV.19 obviously does not fully tap this dimension of behavior, it might reflect either actual upward or downward mobility that is correctly perceived by the respondent or a perverse self-aggrandizing or self-effacing tendency, and as such be indicative of some sort of status anxiety. As can be seen from the table, the early Goldwater group scores slightly below the mean percentage of mismatched respondents. Thus, if such mismatching is a measure of status anxiety, it does not support the notion of status anxiety as causally related to political extremism if we accept support for Goldwater as in any sense the equivalent of extremism.

The thesis that equated support for McCarthy with populism, so well refuted by Michael Rogin in his volume on McCarthy,[20] cannot really be tested for its applicability to the Goldwater movement by the data we have here. But it is interesting to note that Goldwater got almost no early support in the New England states and very little in the middle-Atlantic area. He received disproportionate support from the southern and border states and slightly disproportionate early backing in the West (see Table III.10). Although there was no overrepresentation of rural respondents among the early Goldwater group, there was considerable overrepresentation (11 percentage points above the sample as a whole) of persons living in small towns of 2,500 to 9,999 persons. Thus the group did have a slightly small-town, southern cast, but this, of course, is a far cry from being coextensive with even southern populism. As we shall see, members of these geographical groups are vastly overrepresented in the Wallace movement. Finally, members of the early Goldwater group were less likely than members of any of the others to have grown up on a farm and more likely to have come from larger cities of 250,000 or more.

Religious fundamentalism (as reflected in the denomination of church membership), a trait often associated with right-wing political extremism, was not found disproportionately among Goldwater's early supporters. In fact, as we saw in Chapter III, they had the smallest proportion of members in pietistic Protestant and neo-fundamentalist denominations and the largest in the traditionally high-status Reformation Protestant churches—Presbyterian, Episcopal, Lutheran, and the like. They did, however, go to church more often than any other group.

Earlier I mentioned Martin Trow's work on support for McCarthy in Bennington because of the similarity of the early Goldwater sup-

[20]Michael P. Rogin, *The Intellectuals and McCarthy: The Radical Specter* (Cambridge: M.I.T. Press, 1967).

porters to Trow's McCarthy supporters in overrepresentation of small businessmen and self-employed persons. Almost 30 percent of the early Goldwater group was self-employed. About a quarter of the later supporters of the senator were also self-employed, but only 17 percent of Johnson's backers were. Trow's analysis of the political divisions in Bennington led him to construct a fourfold typology of political outlook based on the attitudes of his respondents toward two of the major economic institutions of American society: big business and labor. Trow's four groups were "nineteenth-century liberals," or persons holding unfavorable attitudes toward *both* business and labor (it was in this group that his McCarthy supporters were overwhelmingly located); "right-wing conservatives," or persons holding negative attitudes toward labor and favorable opinions toward business; "moderate conservatives," or respondents with favorable attitudes toward both business and labor; and "labor liberals," the obverse of the right-wing conservatives, who liked labor unions but opposed big business.[21]

Persons were assigned to the various categories in accordance with their responses to questions on business and labor as registered on the feeling thermometer. Respondents who rated both business and labor 49 degrees or lower on the feeling thermometer, for example, were designated as nineteenth-century liberals. As Table IV.20 shows, this group, which Trow found to be so predominantly pro-McCarthy, was not very strongly represented among the supporters of Senator Goldwater. Only 5 percentage points separated the early Goldwater group from the Johnson group on this measure. However, there were many more "right-wing conservatives" among Goldwater's backers (both early and late) than among Johnson's backers. About 27 percentage points separated these groups. There was no substantial difference between the early and late Goldwater groups on this measure, however, so it probably indicates a difference that we would normally expect to find between Republicans and Democrats.

Finally, first Polsby and later Wolfinger and Converse[22] have noted the importance of party identification in the composition of many of America's recent rightist and conservative movements. It may seem that a perfectly circular argument on this point would be the only one possible here because the analytic groups are based on candidate

[21]Trow, "Right-Wing Radicalism."

[22]Nelson W. Polsby, "Toward an Explanation of McCarthyism," in *Politics and Social Life,* ed. Nelson W. Polsby, Robert A. Dentler, and Paul Smith (Boston: Houghton Mifflin, 1963); Raymond E. Wolfinger *et al.,* "America's Radical Right: Politics and Ideology," in *Ideology and Discontent,* ed. David E. Apter (New York: Free Press, Macmillan, 1964); Converse *et al.,* "Electoral Myth and Reality."

TABLE IV.20

Distribution of 1964 Candidate-Preference Groups Among Trow's Four Categories of Political Orientation

	19th-Century Liberals		Moderate Conservatives		Right-Wing Conservatives		Labor Liberals		Total	
	N	%	N	%	N	%	N	%	N	%
Early Goldwater supporters	9	13.2%	27	39.7%	30	44.1%	2	2.9%	68	100.0%
Later Goldwater supporters	12	9.3	54	41.9	56	43.4	7	5.4	129	100.0
Johnson supporters	37	8.2	267	58.9	76	16.8	73	16.1	453	100.0
Undecided and other	21	13.9	79	52.3	34	22.5	17	11.3	151	100.0
Total	79	9.9	427	53.3	196	24.5	99	12.4	801	100.0

Adapted from material in Martin Trow, "Right-Wing Radicalism and Political Intolerance: A Study of Support for McCarthy in a New England Town" (unpublished Ph.D. dissertation, Columbia University, 1957).

preference, and therefore, by extension, on partisan identification. There is some rather convincing evidence, however, that Republicanism (of an independent variety) is an important and almost unique aspect of the early Goldwater group if attitudinal consistency is added as a criterion for right-wing interest-group membership.

In discussing the construction of the candidate-preference groups (see Chapter III) I noted the discrepancy between support for the John Birch Society and inconsistent opposition to groups like labor unions and liberals, the supposedly pro-Birch respondents often being pro-labor and/or pro-liberal. Simple early support for Goldwater was shown to be a better predictor of consistently conservative or rightist attitudes than was the Birch Society question.

And it is most certainly the case that both early and late Goldwater supporters predominantly identified themselves as Republican. There was a greater proportion of Democrats and independent Republicans among the senator's early supporters than among his later backers, but the Republican party is nevertheless the political home of the great majority of Americans who take consistently conservative approaches to political matters. No great wave of right-wing Democrats fell into Goldwater's camp, even though the defection rate from the Democratic party in the South, a trend visible for many years, was larger in 1964 than usual.

We have seen that Goldwaterism was hardly a mass movement in the sense of a sweeping abandonment of political norms and processes, and that in many respects its members were traditionally conservative both in their socioeconomic roles and in their political beliefs. We have examined some evidence that suggests that at least the early Goldwater group showed a reasonably clear-cut set of conservative political values —perhaps a conservative ideology. The charges of extremism and racism directed at Goldwater's followers by liberals have been shown to have some foundations in fact; but at the same time these tendencies among his supporters have been found to a somewhat lesser degree than many commentators seemed to believe in 1964.

What emerges from these data is a portrait of a small but active segment of Republican conservatives, people with strong opinions, money, middle-class status, and education. They committed themselves more heavily than any other group to the election of their candidate in 1964. They did all they could, but their views had virtually no general appeal. That they captured the party at the national level attests to their dedication. If they still retain any measure of control, it is due to their perseverence in the face of the fact that they represent minority opinion both within and without their party.

CHAPTER V

Wallace[1]

WE HAVE SEEN that the evidence for the growth of a large-scale conservative movement in the United States in the period 1960–1964 is
rather weak, and of an extensive right-wing extremist movement even
weaker. The presidential campaign and election of 1968, however,
offered the American people their first opportunity (outside the South)
to support a rightist third-party candidate since the election of 1936,
and therefore serves as a somewhat better test of the strength of rightist
sentiment in the United States than did the election of 1964. In that
campaign, in my estimation, conservatism, not right-wing extremism,
was Goldwater's dominant theme and dominant appeal. In 1968 the
rightist candidate was, of course, George Corley Wallace, who began
his campaign for the presidency early in 1967 and ended it nineteen
months later with almost 14 percent of the popular vote, with the
skeleton of a national party organization, and after alarming both major
parties and the Congress because for a time it seemed possible that he
might throw the election into the House of Representatives.[2]

[1] I would like to acknowledge the assistance of Ralph K. Requa for his help in
the early portions of this chapter.

[2] Wallace's hope of throwing the election into the House rested on the premise that
he might prevent either major candidate from obtaining the necessary 270 electoral votes for the election. Wallace proposed to do this by winning in the South
and by dividing the vote in several key border and northern states so that he
would get a plurality of the votes in each of these states and thereby all its
electoral votes. This latter strategy required that a voting pattern of 34–33–33
percent, or a variation still yielding a Wallace plurality, would occur in these
key states. Wallace carried five states, winning a total of 46 electoral votes and
13.49 percent of the popular vote, or 9,898,543 votes, of which 5,072,554 were
in the South. Wallace received 34.3 percent of the total southern vote and
8.24 percent of the total nonsouthern vote.

Although Wallace, like Goldwater, was widely advertised as an extremist, this label was hardly the point of debate that it had been in 1964, perhaps because he was a third-party candidate and was so openly identified with totalitarianism generally and with hostility to civil rights and integration in particular. Nevertheless, if a consensus existed among elites and in the mass public that Wallace was an extremist, a significant minority of the population was not thereby deterred from support-ing him.

Wallace, while broadly judged by his opposition as a racist pure and simple, in fact organized his campaign around several issues not directly related to race. Foremost among these, of course, was his con-tinual insistence, with obvious populist overtones, that he was deter-mined to right the repeated injustices of a vast and corrupt federal bureaucracy against the "little people." In addition he argued that his campaign was "necessary" since the Republican and Democratic parties were "no different than Tweedledum and Tweedledee," and offered neither a choice nor an echo to the voters, who, he asserted, were

with me, who stand for things I stand for, [who] couldn't vote for any of them [candidates of the major parties]. There's not a dime's worth of dif-ference in the way the leaders of both parties think. They've been guilty of the same high crimes and misdemeanors—both parties have encroached on states' rights, on property ownership, on private enterprise.[3]

And people are resentful . . . toward the solution of all problems with more federal force and more take-over of individual liberty and freedom.[4]

On almost every major social issue of the 1968 election, Wallace took positions directly opposing those of the major parties. He stood for, as he said, law and order, but also for reorganizing the U.N., which he said "wasn't worth much,"[5] and for a very heavy reliance on the Joint Chiefs of Staff for help in formulating military and foreign policy, and of course he was strongly opposed to open-housing legislation, the integration of schools by busing or any other means, and the imple-mentation of the various civil rights acts passed by Congress in the past fifteen years.

In so brief a scope as this, it is difficult to describe fully the issues upon which Wallace based his campaign, but the following statement, I think, covers much of the overt rationale for his candidacy:

I have traveled throughout our country in the last year, literally from Concord, New Hampshire, to Los Angeles, California, to Miami, Florida.

[3]*Saturday Evening Post,* June 15, 1968, p. 24.
[4]*U.S. News and World Report,* June 1, 1964, p. 63.
[5]Reprinted by Wallace for President Committee, June 1968, from the *Birming-ham News* (n.d.).

The American people are hungry for a change in the direction of our national government. They are concerned and disturbed about the trends being followed by our national leadership.

Today our country pursues a foreign policy which gains neither the respect of our friends or our enemies.

The domestic policies of our nation's government have caused our people to become a government-fearing rather than a God-fearing people.

We must have a country whose leadership instills in its people a sense of national pride.

We must have a national leadership which does not condone and explain away lawlessness. The typical American of all races is tired of riots—of crime running rampant in every city of our nation.

Our national government—the executive, the judicial, the legislative—must go by the Constitution of the United States.

We must have a nation wherein our states are able to run their affairs, their schools, hospitals and other domestic institutions without receiving directives from Washington, D.C.

We must have a nation which will not tolerate defiance of its national security by those within who offer aid and comfort to our enemies. I want treasonable acts punished.

We have a nation which has fed, clothed and rehabilitated its allies for many years. We must have a national leadership which tells those allies: "We are not going to be the bulwark against communist aggression all over the world and have you sit idly by while the youth and strength of our country is sapped away. If we go, you go with us." The American people are tired of allies who take from us but refuse to assist us in the preservation of freedom. We must have a nation whose fighting men and their families know that there is direction and a reason for their daily commitment between life and death.

We must have a nation where the free enterprise system is left alone and allowed to work. Labor union members, small businesses, and large ones, too, are tired of having to keep books for the federal government. Government interference stifles the free enterprise system and the growth of our gross national product more than any other single thing.

We must have concern for the American farmer and understand that he should receive his fair share of the food dollar.

We must have a national leadership which defends, not destroys, the right of ownership of private property.

There has been no response from either of the parties which would show the American people that they are heeding the growing disillusionment with what amounts to a one-party system in the United States. No prospective candidate of the two existing parties, nor anyone in party leadership position, has come forward with any indication that there will be any difference in their platforms. No one has suggested that the wishes of the American people will be heard.

So today, I state to you that I am a candidate for the President of the United States.[6]

Race (which, significantly, is not even mentioned in this announcement of his candidacy), loss of national prestige, free enterprise, opposition to federal power, and crime in the streets were the themes to which Wallace would return again and again in his campaign.

In searching for the causes of support for Wallace, one is pulled in two theoretical directions. The first of these, discussed earlier in connection with support for Goldwater, is derived from theories of political extremism and is, as I noted, based in the research traditions of mass-society theory and authoritarianism; the second is drawn from political science and concerns the origins of third parties. The most comprehensive formulation of third-party theory appears in *The American Voter's* discussion of agrarian political behavior and in Converse's article "Information Flow and the Stability of Partisan Attitudes" in *Elections and the Political Order*.[7] A brief review may be useful:

The theory advanced in *The American Voter* rests on the assertion that there is, as I discussed earlier, a causal relationship among economic sensitivity, low political involvement, and support for a third party. Groups that are highly sensitive to economic fluctuations and at the same time are not generally integrated into voluntary associations, lack political information, have weak affective ties to political parties, and have low levels of political involvement are likely, when economic recession or depression strikes, to support third parties. Such a party is formed by an elite whose motivations and ideologies may or may not be representative of the beliefs of the eventual mass base of the movement. Examples are the People's party, the Non Partisan League, and the like.

Although these theories converge on the importance of low levels of information and weak attachments to the political system as determinants of support for third parties, they diverge somewhat on the issues of the relative importance of social-class position, the influence

[6]American Independent party campaign leaflet (Sacramento, Calif., 1968). See the *Congressional Quarterly's* publication *Candidates 1968*, pp. 89–95, for a brief review of Wallace's life and political career. The best biography so far is *Wallace* by Marshall Frady (New York: New American Library, 1968). Robert Sherrill's *Gothic Politics in the Deep South* (New York: Ballantine Books, 1960) has an interesting chapter (pp. 302–67) on Wallace's career. There were, of course, numerous campaign publications, many taking the form of published questions and answers. See, for example, John J. Synon, ed., *George Wallace: Profile of a Presidential Candidate* (Kilmarnock, Va.: MS, Inc., 1968).

[7]Angus Campbell et al., *The American Voter* (New York: Wiley, 1960), chap. 15, and Philip E. Converse, "Information Flow and the Stability of Partisan Attitudes," in *Elections and the Political Order*, ed. Angus Campbell et al. (New York: Wiley, 1967).

TABLE V.1

Demographic Characteristics of Candidate-Preference Groups, 1968

	Wallace Supporters		Humphrey Supporters		Nixon Supporters		Undecided and Other		Total	
	N	%	N	%	N	%	N	%	N	%
AGE										
21–23	5	3.2%	8	1.9%	15	2.9%	7	5.0%	35	2.8%
24–26	12	7.8	24	5.6	16	3.1	6	4.3	58	4.7
27–29	13	8.4	20	4.7	36	6.9	6	4.3	75	6.0
30–34	9	5.8	38	8.8	43	8.3	10	7.1	100	8.0
35–39	24	15.6	43	10.0	40	7.7	12	8.5	119	9.6
40–49	36	23.4	104	24.2	122	23.5	44	31.2	306	24.6
50–64	41	26.6	112	26.0	142	27.3	33	23.4	328	26.3
65 and over	14	9.1	81	18.8	106	20.4	23	16.3	224	18.0
Total	154	100.0%	430	100.0%	520	100.0%	141	100.0%	1,245	100.0%
SEX										
Male	91	59.1%	178	41.1%	239	45.8%	66	46.8%	574	45.9%
Female	63	40.9	255	58.9	283	54.2	75	53.2	676	54.1
Total	154	100.0%	433	100.0%	522	100.0%	141	100.0%	1,250	100.0%
RACE										
White	151	98.1%	319	73.7%	515	98.7%	135	95.7%	1,120	89.6%
Negro	1	0.6	106	24.5	3	.6	5	3.5	115	9.2
Other	2	1.2	8	1.9	4	.8	1	.7	15	1.2
Total	154	100.0%	433	100.0%	522	100.0%	141	100.0%	1,250	100.0%
REGION										
Northeast	20	13.0%	117	27.0%	137	26.2%	34	24.1%	308	24.6%
Midwest	38	24.7	135	31.2	179	34.3	47	33.3	399	31.9
South	82	53.2	118	27.3	115	22.0	36	25.5	351	28.1
West	14	9.1	63	14.5	91	17.4	24	17.0	192	15.4
Total	154	100.0%	433	100.0%	522	100.0%	141	100.0%	1,250	100.0%

EDUCATION										
Grade school	37	24.0%	119	27.5%	70	13.4%	28	20.0%	254	20.4%
Some high school	33	21.4	77	17.8	82	15.7	19	13.6	211	16.9
High school graduate	50	32.5	145	33.6	173	33.2	57	40.7	425	34.0
Some college	24	15.6	42	9.7	93	17.9	23	16.4	182	14.7
College graduate	10	6.5	49	11.3	103	19.8	13	9.3	175	14.0
Total	154	100.0%	432	100.0%	521	100.0%	140	100.0%	1,247	100.0%
OCCUPATION (head of household)										
Professional and technical	14	9.1%	53	12.2%	118	22.6%	18	12.8%	203	16.2%
Managers and officials	25	16.2	47	10.9	87	16.7	19	13.5	178	14.2
Clerical and kindred workers	13	8.4	36	8.3	45	8.6	10	7.1	104	8.3
Craftsmen, firemen	43	27.9	79	18.2	108	20.7	37	26.2	267	21.4
Operatives	27	17.5	84	19.4	55	10.5	29	20.6	195	15.6
Household and service workers	8	5.2	40	9.2	13	2.5	3	2.1	64	5.1
Laborers (nonfarm)	4	2.6	12	2.8	12	2.3	3	2.1	31	2.5
Farmers	8	5.2	22	5.1	25	4.8	6	4.3	61	4.9
Farm laborers	11	7.1	34	7.9	41	7.9	11	7.8	97	7.8
Other	1	.6	26	6.0	18	3.4	5	3.5	50	4.0
Total	154	100.0%	433	100.0%	522	100.0%	141	100.0%	1,250	100.0%
INCOME (combined family)										
0–$3,999	25	16.5%	102	24.6%	80	15.7%	28	20.0%	235	19.3%
$4,000–5,999	19	12.6	51	12.3	62	12.2	20	14.3	152	12.5
$6,000–7,999	41	27.2	74	17.8	92	18.1	28	20.0	235	19.4
$8,000–9,999	19	12.6	53	12.8	73	14.4	21	15.0	166	13.7
$10,000–14,000	28	18.5	95	22.9	116	22.8	31	22.1	270	22.3
$15,000 and over	19	12.6	39	9.4	85	16.7	12	8.6	155	12.7
Total	151	100.0%	414	100.0%	508	100.0%	140	100.0%	1,213	100.0%

TABLE V.1 (Continued)

	Wallace Supporters		Humphrey Supporters		Nixon Supporters		Undecided and Other		Total	
	N	%	N	%	N	%	N	%	N	%
PLACE BROUGHT UP										
Farm	64	43.0%	106	26.0%	152	29.8%	47	35.1%	369	30.8%
Town	40	26.8	127	31.2	148	29.0	32	23.9	347	28.9
Small city	12	8.1	58	14.2	81	15.8	24	17.9	175	14.0
Large city	33	22.1	116	28.5	129	25.3	31	23.1	309	25.8
Total	149	100.0%	407	100.0%	510	100.0%	134	100.0%	1,200	100.0%
SIZE OF CITY OF RESIDENCE										
Metropolitan area*	8	5.2%	76	18.1%	36	6.9%	10	7.1%	130	10.4%
50,000 and over	30	19.5	88	21.0	91	17.4	26	18.4	235	18.9
10,000–49,999	20	13.0	81	19.3	119	22.8	27	19.1	247	19.8
2,500–9,999	36	23.4	82	19.5	115	22.0	33	23.4	266	21.3
Rural area	60	39.0	93	22.1	161	30.8	45	31.9	359	29.7
Total	154	100.0%	420	100.0%	522	100.0%	141	100.0%	1,237	100.0%
MARITAL STATUS										
Married	122	79.2%	303	70.0%	383	73.5%	100	70.9%	908	72.6%
Single	10	6.5	33	7.6	46	8.8	16	11.3	105	8.4
Divorced	7	4.5	25	5.8	23	4.4	5	3.5	60	4.8
Separated	1	.6	16	3.7	3	.6	4	2.8	24	1.9
Widowed	14	9.1	56	12.9	66	12.6	16	11.3	152	12.2
Total	154	100.0%	433	100.0%	521	100.0%	141	100.0%	1,249	100.0%

*Central cities of twelve largest standard metropolitan statistical areas.

of ideology, and the significance of social and psychological pathology as determinants of third-party voting.

In Chapter II I argued that there is a reasonably close fit between this theory of third parties (the marginal-participant theory) and the empirical evidence that I reviewed about the American right from the McCarthy period forward. The direct application of this theory to the Goldwater movement is, of course, wholly inappropriate.

The Wallace movement, however, provides the first opportunity to test the marginal-participant theory with national survey data collected from a major third party's mass base. Unfortunately, certain problems with temporal causal sequences make the available data somewhat less than ideal for this test. On the other hand, they are not altogether useless.

Because of the importance of demographic variables in the analysis of both of these theories, it is appropriate at this point to examine Table V.1. What seems most interesting here is the general dispersion of Wallace supporters among the lower and middle strata of the population. Wallace supporters have a tendency to be less educated than the other candidate-preference groups and are particularly underrepresented in the higher educational strata, having only half as many college graduates, proportionately, as Humphrey's supporters, and a third as many as Nixon's. Their income distributions and occupations, however, are rather similar to those of the rest of the sample.

One important demographic question that is not answered by these data is the degree to which southern birth and socialization, followed by out-migration, were responsible for the Wallace vote outside the South. That is, were Wallace supporters in the North and West simply transplanted southerners? The answer to this question is found in Table V.2. As this table indicates, just slightly more than 10 percent of Wallace's supporters outside the South were born in southern or border states, a figure slightly smaller than the proportion of Humphrey backers from these areas (many of whom were Negro) and just slightly larger than the proportion of Nixon's supporters from the same regions. Thus the out-migration hypothesis is not sustained, and therefore tabulations in which a control for region is appropriate will be based on region of residence in 1968, when the data were gathered. In some cases, however, I will not report bivariate distributions with this control. Instead, the regional control will be applied to the multivariate models of Wallace support which appear at the end of this chapter (Figures V.2 and V.3). There, simultaneous controls are applied to all of the variables in the models, and the control for residence is introduced through the device of developing a model for the South and another for the rest of the nation. By comparing the two models it is possible to determine

TABLE V.2
Place of Birth of Supporters of 1968 Candidates
Currently Residing Outside of South

| | *Place of Birth* | | | | | | | |
| | *Nonsouth* | | *South* | | *Border* | | *Total* | |
	N	%	N	%	N	%	N	%
Wallace supporters	63	88.7%	7	9.9%	1	1.4%	71	100.0%
Humphrey supporters	267	85.6	37	11.9	8	2.6	312	100.0
Nixon supporters	373	92.1	15	3.7	17	4.2	405	100.0
Undecided and other	97	92.4	6	5.7	2	1.9	105	100.0
Total	800	89.6	65	7.3	28	3.1	893	100.0

rather readily the overall effect of any given variable on support for Wallace in either region. And, as one might suspect, there are some marked differences between Wallace supporters in the South and those living in other parts of the country.

Finally, it is also worth observing that about 25 percent of Wallace's supporters consisted of people between the ages of twenty-one and thirty-four, compared with approximately 21 percent of the total sample in this age range, indicating slightly disproportionate support for Wallace among younger persons.

MARGINAL PARTICIPATION:
A TEST OF THIRD-PARTY THEORY

Let us now consider the marginal-voter theory. It is unfortunate that the critical tests of the application of this theory to the Wallace movement are seriously restricted and compromised by the presumption that the political habits and opinions of Wallace supporters had developed before Wallace himself appeared on the political scene and an interviewer arrived to collect data on them. The factors precipitating a voter's movement into Wallace's column may at the same time or earlier have heightened his sensitivity to political matters generally, propelled him into campaign work for the first time, started him thinking about the other parties, and so on. The effect, then, of being a Wallace supporter may mask normally quiescent and apathetic responses to questions about political activity, efficacy, and involvement, temporarily (but for the moment accurately) giving the analyst the impression that political zealots are more numerous than casual participants in the movement.

On the other hand, if we can demonstrate that the level of involvement, history of partisan stability, political attention, political activity, and the like are disproportionately weaker in the Wallace supporters even when they are presumably at the height of involvement with their movement, we are making a fairly rigorous test of the theory, because we are adding disadvantages to the test, not advantages. What do our data show us on these points?

About 62 percent of Wallace's supporters resided in areas of less than 10,000 population, compared with 51 percent of the population as a whole (see Table V.1). Even larger and more impressive differences, however, are found in the proportion of Wallace voters brought up on farms: 43 percent compared with 30 percent of the sample. This distinction is, however, a reflection of the heavy southern cast of Wallace support.

An examination of these data by region of residence in 1968 shows that Wallace supporters *outside* the South were essentially no different from the remainder of the sample of voters in the proportion brought up on farms. Nevertheless, southern Wallace supporters were more likely to have been born on farms than southern supporters of either Nixon or Humphrey. Just a little more than half (53.7 percent) of southern Wallace supporters were born on farms; 42.4 percent of Humphrey's backers in the South were of farm origin; and 35.7 percent of Nixon's supporters were born on farms. Thus, while the regional basis of this finding must be recognized, it still gives some support to the marginal-participant theory (in the South) because of the fact that previous research (reported in *The American Voter*) shows that low levels of involvement and participation persist in persons of farm origin, even though they may move later to an urban environment. Therefore, even though we may find southern Wallace supporters of rural origins to be politically active and involved in this campaign, we might, on the basis of previous evidence, infer that this is possibly an abnormal condition and that political quiescence among these persons is the usual state of affairs.[8]

There is some other information that bears indirectly on this point. The responses to the Legitimacy of Government Index reported in Table V.3 show that Wallace supporters as a group are more than twice as likely as any other candidate-preference group to score at the extremely low end of the index and almost twice as likely to be at the

[8]Campbell *et al., American Voter,* p. 412.

TABLE V.3

Scores of Candidate-Preference Groups on Legitimacy of Government Index (LGI), 1968

	LGI Scores*										
	Low				Medium		High				Total	
	1		2		3		4		5			
	N	%	N	%	N	%	N	%	N	%	N	%
Wallace supporters	25	22.7%	39	35.5%	27	24.5%	17	15.5%	2	1.8%	110	100.0%
Humphrey supporters	22	6.7	62	19.0	106	32.4	126	38.5	11	3.4	327	100.0
Nixon supporters	37	9.5	67	17.2	129	33.1	143	36.7	14	3.6	390	100.0
Undecided and other	10	10.7	15	16.1	29	31.2	37	40.0	2	2.0	93	100.0
Total	94	10.2	183	19.9	291	31.6	323	35.1	29	3.2	920	100.0

*See Appendix for index items.

next lowest level of the measure. How are we to interpret this finding? On the one hand, these data may indicate that Wallace supporters hold an enduring distrust of the government and therefore might be presumed to be relatively more detached from the American political system than other voters. If this is true, these data give some support to the marginal-participant theory. It seems equally likely, however, that these responses may reflect short-term opposition to the government's policies in areas like civil rights, and that if these policies were changed, Wallace supporters might then support political institutions and governmental structures. What is obvious, in any case, is that these data indicate relatively greater detachment and alienation from the political system in 1968 among Wallace's backers than among other voters, and therefore, I believe, they are correctly interpreted as supporting the marginal-participant theory if wide variation in the strength of attachment to the political system is acceptable as one indicator of political marginality.

This same general pattern is repeated in the distribution of scores on the Legitimacy of Political Institutions Index (Table V.4). The items in this index include questions like "How much do you feel that having elections makes the government pay attention to what people think?" This table presents the same problems of interpretation as Table V.3, except that I believe a stronger case can be made for interpreting the rather higher rejection of political institutions on the part of the pro-Wallace group as some evidence of disproportionate political marginality.

TABLE V.4

Scores of Candidate-Preference Groups on Legitimacy of Political Institutions Index (LPI), 1968

| | *LPI Scores** | | | | | | | |
| | *Low* | | *Medium* | | *High* | | *Total* | |
	N	%	N	%	N	%	N	%
Wallace supporters	25	20.7%	65	53.7%	31	25.6%	121	100.0%
Humphrey supporters	42	12.4	149	43.8	149	43.8	340	100.0
Nixon supporters	46	10.8	174	40.9	206	48.4	426	100.0
Undecided and other	15	15.0	47	47.0	38	38.0	100	100.0
Total	128	12.9	435	44.0	424	43.0	987	100.0

*Based on a trichotomy of an original index range of 0–8.

All of these measures of legitimacy, like the data on rural origins, are somewhat influenced by the presence of large numbers of southerners in the Wallace column. But in general to impose a control for residence at the time of the survey merely attenuates the differences among the groups; it does not eliminate them entirely, and in some cases it has no effect at all. For example, when the LPI index is applied to regional groups, we find just over a quarter (27.4 percent) of Wallace's supporters in the South to be in the upper third of this index. Their nonsouthern counterparts were only slightly below this level (23.8 percent). In this case, southern influence is expressed in relatively greater belief in the legitimacy of political institutions. Both southern and nonsouthern Wallace supporters, however, assigned much less legitimacy to political institutions than other respondents, regardless of region. In the South, 47 percent of the total sample scored in the upper third of the index; 41.3 percent of the nonsouthern respondents were at this level.

The Political Attention Index, reported in Table V.5, is based on direct questions about how much attention the respondent says he gives to foreign, national, state, and local political affairs. Wallace supporters are very much like the other groups on this measure, and insofar as this attention is independent of their involvement with Wallace, this finding must be seen as contradictory to the marginal-voter theory, since we

TABLE V.5

Scores of Candidate-Preference Groups on Political Attention Index (PAI), 1968

	*PAI Scores**							
	Low		*Medium*		*High*		*Total*	
	N	*%*	*N*	*%*	*N*	*%*	*N*	*%*
Wallace supporters	10	8.9%	57	50.9%	45	40.1%	112	100.0%
Humphrey supporters	25	7.8	146	45.8	148	46.4	319	100.0
Nixon supporters	21	5.0	192	46.3	202	48.7	415	100.0
Undecided and other	6	6.1	52	53.1	40	40.8	98	100.0
Total	62	6.6	447	47.3	435	46.1	944	100.0

*See Appendix for index items.

TABLE V.6

Voting Stability of Candidate-Preference Groups by Level of Education, 1968

Voting Patterns	Wallace Supporters		Humphrey Supporters		Nixon Supporters		Undecided and Other		Total	
	N	%	N	%	N	%	N	%	N	%
LESS THAN 4 YEARS OF HIGH SCHOOL										
Always same	22	66.6%	78	74.3%	28	43.1%	9	32.1%	137	59.3%
Mostly same	2	6.1	2	1.9	6	9.2	5	17.9	15	6.5
Different	9	27.3	25	23.8	31	47.7	14	50.0	79	34.2
Total	33	100.0%	105	100.0%	65	100.0%	28	100.0%	231	100.0%
HIGH SCHOOL GRADUATE OR SOME COLLEGE										
Always same	31	37.8%	155	68.0%	127	42.3%	50	58.1%	363	52.2%
Mostly same	3	3.7	10	4.4	13	4.3	2	2.3	28	4.0
Different	48	58.5	63	27.6	160	53.3	34	39.5	305	43.8
Total	82	100.0%	228	100.0%	300	100.0%	86	100.0%	696	100.0%
COLLEGE GRADUATE OR MORE										
Always same	5	50.0%	27	64.3%	43	45.3%	2	16.7%	77	48.4%
Mostly same	1	10.0	0	0.0	6	6.3	1	8.3	8	5.1
Different	4	40.0	15	35.7	46	48.4	9	75.0	74	46.5
Total	10	100.0%	42	100.0%	95	100.0%	12	100.0%	159	100.0%

TABLE V.7

Voting History of Candidate-Preference Groups, 1968

| | All | | Presidential Elections for Which Respondents Were Eligible in Which They Voted | | | | | | Total | |
| | | | Most | | Some | | None | | | |
	N	%	N	%	N	%	N	%	N	%
Wallace supporters	75	51.7%	34	23.4%	22	15.2%	14	9.7%	145	100.0%
Humphrey supporters	243	59.3	83	20.2	62	15.1	22	5.4	410	100.0
Nixon supporters	326	65.5	110	22.1	42	8.4	20	4.0	498	100.0
Undecided and other	78	58.6	29	21.8	15	11.3	11	8.3	133	100.0
Total	722	60.9	256	21.6	141	11.9	67	5.6	1,186	100.0

TABLE V.8

Strength of Party Identification of Candidate-Preference Groups, 1968

	Strong Democrat		Not Very Strong Democrat		Independent Democrat		Independent		Independent Republican		Not Very Strong Republican		Strong Republican		Total	
	N	%	N	%	N	%	N	%	N	%	N	%	N	%	N	%
Wallace supporters	23	15.0%	49	31.9%	23	15.0%	27	17.6%	16	10.5%	12	7.8%	3	1.9%	153	100.0%
Humphrey supporters	220	50.8	136	31.4	44	10.2	13	3.0	4	.9	15	3.5	1	.2	433	100.0
Nixon supporters	15	2.9	66	12.6	26	5.0	46	8.8	82	15.7	153	29.3	134	25.7	522	100.0
Undecided and other	16	11.5	56	39.9	18	12.9	26	18.5	10	7.2	13	9.3	1	.7	140	100.0
Total	274	22.0	307	24.6	111	8.9	112	9.0	112	9.0	193	15.4	139	11.1	1,248	100.0

would expect lower levels of attention from politically marginal persons, particularly attention to foreign affairs.

There are some additional data, however, that support the marginal-participant theory. Wallace supporters at the middle educational level exceed the party variability of all the other groups and report that they have been less likely to vote in presidential elections than even the undecided voters (see Tables V.6 and V.7). Other tabulations show that they also rank second highest among those who report having "not much" interest in the campaign. Furthermore, as Table V.8 shows, they report that they are independents, independent Republicans, or independent Democrats more often than any of the other groups, with the single exception of Nixon backers, 15.7 percent of whom claim "independent Republican" status.

The groups' levels of political efficacy and political activity are also of interest (see Tables V.9 and V.10). Wallace supporters have a *very low sense of political efficacy* but an average rate of political activity. Why the presence of a third-party candidate and a level of political activity that may be unusually high for this group did not increase its sense of political efficacy is perplexing, because we so often find rather strong positive associations between these two variables.

There are at least two possible interpretations of this finding. It may simply be that the efficacy index measured the preceived legitimacy of the government at the time of the survey. Since this was so low among Wallace supporters—and apparently still is—we may merely be seeing further manifestations of their hostility to governmental policies that played a large part in bringing about their participation in the Wallace movement. On the other hand, if the efficacy scale in fact measures long-term cognitive relationships with the political system, the fact that efficacy had not risen to an average level among Wallace's supporters suggests that they may have been marginal participants in this system prior to the Wallace campaign. Unfortunately, I see no easy resolution of this question.

I do not believe that these data can be interpreted as either strongly supporting or rejecting the marginal-voter hypothesis as applied to the Wallace movement. The best support for the theory comes from the high rate of rural origin of southern Wallace supporters and the relatively weak party identifications of this group, regardless of residence at the time of the survey. But the first of these findings is, of course, based on inferences from previous data and may not in fact apply here at all. Some further support for the theory is also present in the data indicating higher rates of party variability, lower reported turnout rates, and lower levels of interest in the campaign among Wallace's supporters.

TABLE V.9

Political Efficacy Scores of Candidate-Preference Groups (ICPR Index), 1968

	Political Efficacy Scores										
	Low		*Lower Medium*		*Medium*		*Upper Medium*		*High*		*Total*	
	N	%	N	%	N	%	N	%	N	%	N	%
Wallace supporters	29	20.9%	46	33.1%	41	29.5%	16	11.5%	7	5.0%	139	100.0
Humphrey supporters	59	15.1	98	25.1	104	26.6	85	21.7	45	11.5	391	100.0
Nixon supporters	47	9.9	116	24.4	131	27.5	107	22.5	75	15.8	476	100.0
Undecided and other	20	18.2	27	24.5	28	25.5	24	21.8	11	10.0	110	100.0
Total	155	13.9	287	25.7	304	27.2	232	20.8	138	12.4	1,116	100.0

TABLE V.10

Political Activity of Candidate-Preference Groups, by Educational Level, 1968

	Political Activity Scores							
	Low		*Medium*		*High*		*Total*	
	N	%	N	%	N	%	N	%
LESS THAN 4 YEARS OF HIGH SCHOOL								
Wallace supporters	26	89.7%	2	6.9%	1	3.4%	29	100.0%
Humphrey supporters	85	83.3	15	14.7	2	2.0	102	100.0
Nixon supporters	57	89.0	6	9.4	1	1.6	64	100.0
Undecided and other	23	95.5	1	4.5	0	0.0	24	100.0
Total	191	87.2	24	11.0	4	1.8	219	100.0
HIGH SCHOOL GRADUATE OR SOME COLLEGE								
Wallace supporters	67	75.3	18	20.2	4	4.5	89	100.0
Humphrey supporters	177	76.3	48	20.7	7	3.0	232	100.0
Nixon supporters	223	74.9	59	19.8	16	5.3	298	100.0
Undecided and other	72	86.8	10	12.0	1	1.2	83	100.0
Total	539	76.8	135	19.2	28	4.0	702	100.0
COLLEGE GRADUATE OR MORE								
Wallace supporters	4	57.1	3	42.9	0	0.0	7	100.0
Humphrey supporters	23	52.3	16	36.3	5	11.4	44	100.0
Nixon supporters	54	58.7	27	29.4	11	12.0	92	100.0
Undecided and other	7	70.0	3	30.0	0	0.0	10	100.0
Total	88	59.5	45	34.7	16	5.8	153	100.0

I have argued that it is possible to construe the responses of this group to the indices of efficacy, legitimacy of government, and legitimacy of political institutions as indicative of detachment or marginality. However, I do not think the case is very strong. The problem, of course, is that it is difficult if not impossible to separate the short-term influence of involvement with Wallace—which has the effect of inflating political interest and activity on the part of Wallace supporters—from long-term political participation and involvement. We might be able to devise other measures of marginality, perhaps by coding the candidate evaluation questions to produce a measure of mass, as described by Philip Converse.[9] If mass were to be significantly lower among Wallace supporters than among other candidate-preference groups (when appropriate demographic controls were applied to the data), this would be evidence in favor of the marginal-participant theory. Unfortunately, I do not have such data available for consideration at this time.

[9]Converse, "Information Flow."

STATUS DISCREPANCY AND POLITICAL ORIENTATION

Let us now consider the theories of right-wing extremist behavior that were examined in the analysis of Goldwater supporters. Table V.11 shows the proportion of each candidate-preference group in four of several possible objective (i.e., stratification-based) situations of status discrepancy. As this table shows, there was little difference in status discrepancy between Wallace supporters and the other groups, a situation that parallels our earlier analysis of Goldwater backers. I do not insist that the tests of the status discrepancy hypothesis that I have presented thus far are necessarily the best that could be devised; indeed, they may be too "difficult," i.e., more substantial imbalances might be discovered if less extreme measures of occupation, income, and education were employed. I therefore computed correlations between two of these three variables (income and education) for each of the candidate-preference groups in order to see if there were greater objective differences among the groups when all respondents were included in the test. I found that the correlation between income and education for Wallace's backers was .436, for Humphrey's supporters .475, for Nixon's supporters .445, and for the undecided voters .452. These coefficients do not argue very strongly for any very serious discrepancies between the income and educational levels of the individuals in these groups. Perhaps one or more of my readers will wish to pursue the application of the status discrepancy theory (based on objective imbalances) to contemporary rightist political

TABLE V.11

Status Discrepancy as Shown by Comparison of Occupation, Income, and Educational Attainment Among Candidate-Preference Groups, 1968
(In Percentages)

	Grade School Education and Income > $10,000	Grade School Education and Upper White-Collar Occupation	At Least Some College and Blue-Collar Occupation	Blue-Collar Occupation and Income > $10,000
Wallace supporters	2.6%	2.6%	2.6%	2.6%
Humphrey supporters	2.8	2.1	3.7	5.1
Nixon supporters	1.3	2.1	5.2	1.9
Undecided and other	0.0	0.7	5.7	4.3

TABLE V.12

Distribution of 1968 Candidate-Preference Groups Among
Trow's Four Categories of Political Orientation
(In Percentages)

	19th-Century Liberals	*Moderate Conservatives*	*Right-Wing Conservatives*	*Labor Liberals*
Wallace supporters	6.2%	51.9%	28.4%	13.6%
Humphrey supporters	9.0	60.7	12.8	17.5
Nixon supporters	10.6	47.6	35.4	6.3
Undecided and other	14.9	58.1	17.6	9.5

Adapted from material in Martin Trow, "Right-Wing Radicalism and Political Intolerance: A Study of Support for McCarthy in a New England Town" (unpublished Ph.D. dissertation, Columbia University, 1957).

movements in somewhat greater detail. I do not believe that the theory has proven of any explanatory value in the case of either the Wallace or the Goldwater movement, however, and I am therefore more than willing to leave to others any further investigation of the significance of this theory as a possible cause of rightist political behavior at the mass level.

As you may recall, Trow found the sample of McCarthy supporters he studied in Bennington to be disproportionately hostile to both organized labor and big business—a position he termed "nineteenth-century liberalism."[10] In 1964 there was a heavy concentration of Goldwater Republicans in the group he termed "right-wing conservatives" (those approving of big business and hostile to labor), but in 1968 all the candidate-preference groups fell predominantly in the "moderate conservatives" column, and there was no particular orientation that distinguished Wallace supporters from the other groups (see Table V.12). There were fewer "right-wing conservatives" among them than among Nixon supporters, but they also included more than twice as many "labor liberals" as the Nixon backers did.

SOCIAL STATUS AND CLASS IDENTIFICATION

The demographic data reviewed earlier show that the Wallace movement was largely southern based and made up of persons of rural

[10]Martin Trow, "Right-Wing Radicalism and Political Intolerance: A Study of Support for McCarthy in a New England Town" (unpublished Ph.D. dissertation, Columbia University, 1957).

origins who were living in small cities or rural areas in 1968. This suggests a strong working-class component to the movement, and indeed this is the case. Sixty-three percent of Wallace supporters identified themselves as belonging to the working class, compared with 57.6 percent of Humphrey's backers and 40.2 percent of Nixon's. Wallace partisans also expressed somewhat greater feelings of class solidarity than the other candidate-preference groups, but were not very different from Humphrey's supporters in this respect (42.2 percent of the Wallace backers and 37.2 percent of the Humphrey group said they felt close or very close to their class of identification).

A rough indication of the intergenerational mobility of persons in both middle and working classes in 1968 is found in Table V.13. As this table indicates, among middle-class respondents there was a very slight tendency for Wallace supporters to have experienced less upward intergenerational mobility than backers of Humphrey or Nixon, and a slightly lower rate of intergenerational mobility prevailed among Wallace partisans in the working class.

WALLACE AND RELIGIOUS FUNDAMENTALISM

Many observers have suggested that there is a causal (and probably reciprocal) relationship between religious fundamentalism and anti-democratic or extremist political movements. Although, as the data in

TABLE V.13

Intergenerational Mobility of Candidate-Preference Groups, 1968:
Respondents' and Families' Social-Class Identification
(In Percentages)

	Social-Class Identification		
	Respondents	Respondents' Families	Net Change
MIDDLE-CLASS RESPONDENTS			
Wallace supporters	33.8%	25.3%	+ 8.5
Humphrey supporters	38.6	28.2	+10.6
Nixon supporters	55.8	38.5	+17.3
Undecided and other	44.0	27.7	+16.3
WORKING-CLASS RESPONDENTS			
Wallace supporters	63.0	72.1	− 9.1
Humphrey supporters	57.6	68.1	−10.5
Nixon supporters	40.2	57.3	−17.1
Undecided and other	51.0	62.4	−11.4

TABLE V.14

Religion and Church Attendance of Candidate-Preference Groups, 1968

	Wallace Supporters		Humphrey Supporters		Nixon Supporters		Undecided and Other		Total	
	N	%	N	%	N	%	N	%	N	%
RELIGION										
Catholic	25	16.2%	128	29.6%	93	17.8%	35	24.8%	281	22.5%
Jewish	2	1.3	27	6.2	4	0.8	3	2.1	36	2.9
General Protestants*	7	4.5	9	2.1	23	4.4	2	1.4	41	3.3
Reformation Protestants†	14	9.1	56	12.9	146	28.0	31	22.0	247	19.8
Pietistic Protestants‡	78	50.6	160	37.0	195	37.4	50	35.5	483	38.6
Neo-fundamentalists§	16	10.4	27	6.2	33	6.3	6	4.3	82	6.6
Nontraditional Christian¶	3	1.9	7	1.6	15	2.9	2	1.4	27	2.2
Other	9	5.8	19	4.4	13	2.5	12	8.5	53	4.2
Total	154	100.0%	433	100.0%	522	100.0%	141	100.0%	1,250	100.0%
CHURCH ATTENDANCE										
Regular	46	30.5%	186	43.9%	218	42.5%	45	32.7%	495	40.4%
Often	21	13.9	67	15.8	84	16.4	24	17.4	196	16.0
Seldom	64	42.4	127	30.0	178	34.7	53	38.4	422	34.4
Never	20	13.2	44	10.4	33	6.4	16	11.6	113	9.2
Total	151	100.0%	424	100.0%	513	100.0%	138	100.0%	1,226	100.0%

*Persons responding only "Protestant."

†Presbyterian, Lutheran, Congregational, Evangelical Reformed, Dutch or Christian Reformed, United Church of Christ, Episcopalian, Anglican.

‡Methodist, African Methodist Episcopal, United or Evangelical Brethren, Baptist, Disciples of Christ, Christian.

§United Missionary, Church of God, Nazarene or Free Methodist, Church of God and Christ, Plymouth Brethren, Pentecostal or Assembly of God, Church of Christ, Salvation Army, Primitive Baptist, Free Will Baptist, Southern Baptist, Seventh-Day Adventist, other fundamentalists.

¶Christian Scientist, Spiritualist, Mormon, Unitarian, Jehovah's Witnesses, Quakers, Unity.

TABLE V.15

Candidate-Preference Groups' by Scores on Civil Rights Index,*
by Region of Residence

	Favorable to Civil Rights		Neutral on Civil Rights		Hostile to Civil Rights		Total	
	N	%	N	%	N	%	N	%
SOUTH								
Wallace								
supporters	10	13.0%	11	14.3%	56	72.7%	77	100.0%
Humphrey								
supporters	76	71.0	10	9.3	21	19.6	107	100.0
Nixon								
supporters	28	27.7	.17	16.8	56	55.4	101	100.0
Undecided								
and other	4	14.3	6	21.4	18	64.3	28	100.0
NONSOUTH								
Wallace								
supporters	11	16.7	19	28.8	36	54.5	66	100.0
Humphrey								
supporters	155	59.2	45	17.2	62	23.7	262	100.0
Nixon								
supporters	132	38.4	79	23.0	133	38.7	344	100.0
Undecided								
and other	38	44.7	12	14.1	35	41.2	85	100.0

*Items are found in the Appendix. When blacks are removed from these tabulations, there is a shift in scores by Humphrey supporters as follows: favorable, 53.8 percent; neutral, 17.8 percent; hostile, 28.4 percent. There are only three pro-Nixon blacks and one pro-Wallace black in the sample.

Table V.14 show, Wallace supporters were most likely to be found in the more fundamentalist denominations (pietistic Protestants and neo-fundamentalists), they had at the same time the weakest formal attachments to religion, at least as evidenced by their conspicuously low rate of church attendance. Almost 55 percent of the Wallace backers seldom or never attended church, compared with 42.8 percent of the total sample. Another measure of fundamentalism, agreement with the statement "The Bible is God's word and all it says is true," was nevertheless most often approved by the Wallace group (60 percent versus 51 percent of the total sample), and it is this measure of attitudinal or ideological fundamentalism that is employed in the multivariate models below (Figures V.2 and V.3).

These data argue, I believe, for a religious portrait of Wallace supporters as somewhat anomic orthodox Christians who are disproportionately detached from religious institutions even though they maintain, generally speaking, the Bible-believing and God-fearing faith of classic American fundamentalism.

CIVIL RIGHTS, PREJUDICE, AND SUPPORT FOR WALLACE

Table V.15 presents each candidate-preference group's scores on a civil rights index by region of residence. As we would expect, this table discloses some of the strongest differences to be observed among the groups. Almost three-quarters of Wallace supporters in the South scored at the hostile end of the civil rights index; in the North there was less hostility than in the South, but northern Wallace partisans who were hostile were even more zealous in their opposition to civil rights for Negroes than their southern counterparts.

We saw that it was the northern supporters of Senator Goldwater who were most hostile to Negroes, Jews, and Catholics. Tables V.16

TABLE V.16

Candidate-Preference Groups' Evaluations of Catholics, by Region, 1968
(On Feeling-Thermometer Scale of 100°)

	Negative (<49°)		Neutral (50°–59°)		Positive (>60°)		Total	
	N	%	N	%	N	%	N	%
SOUTH								
Wallace								
supporters	19	24.4%	28	35.9%	31	39.7%	78	100.0%
Humphrey								
supporters	13	11.0	33	28.0	72	61.0	118	100.0
Nixon								
supporters	16	14.2	42	37.2	55	48.7	113	100.0
Undecided								
and other	5	14.7	16	47.1	13	38.2	34	100.0
NONSOUTH								
Wallace								
supporters	9	13.2	19	27.9	40	58.9	68	100.0
Humphrey								
supporters	26	8.6	64	21.1	213	70.3	303	100.0
Nixon								
supporters	34	8.5	119	29.7	248	61.8	401	100.0
Undecided								
and other	8	7.8	27	26.5	67	65.7	102	100.0

TABLE V.17

Candidate-Preference Groups' Evaluations of Jews, by Region, 1968
(On Feeling-Thermometer Scale of 100°)

	Negative (<49°)		Neutral (50°–59°)		Positive (>60°)		Total	
	N	%	N	%	N	%	N	%
SOUTH								
Wallace supporters	12	15.8%	33	43.4%	31	40.8%	76	100.0%
Humphrey supporters	8	6.8	45	38.1	65	55.1	118	100.0
Nixon supporters	4	3.6	43	38.4	65	58.0	112	100.0
Undecided and other	7	20.6	15	44.1	12	35.3	34	100.0
NONSOUTH								
Wallace supporters	10	14.5	27	39.1	32	46.4	69	100.0
Humphrey supporters	13	4.3	85	28.1	205	67.6	303	100.0
Nixon supporters	29	7.3	139	34.8	232	58.0	400	100.0
Undecided and other	7	6.9	44	43.1	51	50.0	102	100.0

through V.18 report the evaluations of Catholics, Jews, and Negroes made by the 1968 candidate-preference groups in the South and in the rest of the country. The pattern of Wallace supporters parallels that of Goldwater's backers, except in the case of Catholics. Outside of the South, Wallace supporters were considerably more hostile to Jews and Negroes than the other candidate-preference groups, and, again with the exception of Catholics, there was little difference between southern and nonsouthern Wallace supporters on these measures.

These data, and those on civil rights reported in Table V.15, support the argument—vigorously denied by Wallace—that racism played a major part in the mobilization of support for his campaign and the American Independent party in 1968. In the only slightly exaggerated words of one Wallace supporter, "When you get right down to it, there's only . . . one issue, and you spell it n-i-g-g-e-r."

Another major issue in the election of 1968 was urban disorder. Since this matter is in large part a racial issue, it seems appropriate to discuss the response of the electorate to this issue in the general

TABLE V.18

Candidate-Preference Groups' Evaluations of Negroes, by Region, 1968
(On Feeling-Thermometer Scale of 100°)

	Negative *(<49°)*		*Neutral* *(50°–59°)*		*Positive* *(>60°)*		*Total*	
	N	*%*	*N*	*%*	*N*	*%*	*N*	*%*
SOUTH								
Wallace								
supporters	19	24.1%	21	26.6%	39	49.4%	79	100.0%
Humphrey								
supporters	3	2.5	14	11.9	101	85.6	118	100.0
Nixon								
supporters	12	10.8	28	25.2	71	64.0	111	100.0
Undecided								
and other	6	17.6	11	32.4	17	50.0	34	100.0
NONSOUTH								
Wallace								
supporters	16	23.2	20	29.0	33	47.8	69	100.0
Humphrey								
supporters	20	6.6	76	25.2	205	68.1	301	100.0
Nixon								
supporters	38	9.5	125	31.4	235	59.0	398	100.0
Undecided								
and other	11	10.9	36	35.6	54	53.5	101	100.0

context of civil rights. In my analysis of these survey data I was unable to find any other variable that so strongly differentiated the candidate-preference groups (although the civil rights measures are a close second) as the issue of urban disorders and ways of dealing with them. Figure V.1 is a simple graph on which I have plotted the positions of the three candidate-preference groups on a seven-point preference scale. A position at the extreme left of the scale indicates that the respondent favored an ameliorative solution to urban disorders: he would try to solve the root causes of the problem. A position at the extreme right of the scale, on the other hand, means that the respondent favored the use of all available military and police force to repress the disorders. It is interesting to observe that the patterns of Wallace and Humphrey supporters are almost perfect mirror images of each other, with Nixon's backers very heavily distributed around the midpoint of the scale. As was the case with the civil rights index, these patterns change if blacks are removed from the computations; 50 percent of Humphrey's sup-

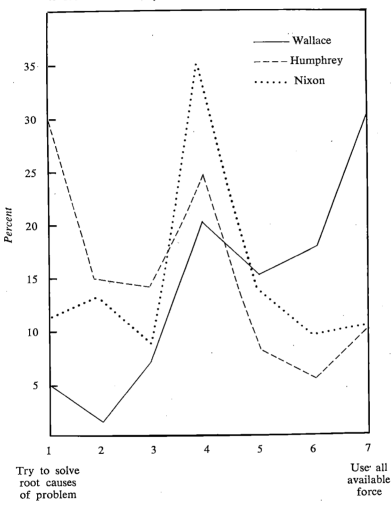

FIGURE V.1

Distributions of Scores on Use of Force as Personally Preferred Solution
to Urban Disorders by Candidate-Preference Groups, 1968

porters then fall on the first three points of the scale, rather than 60
percent. We shall see in the multivariate analysis below that favoring
repression of urban disorders was the single most significant predictor
of support for Wallace outside of the South, and was quite important
in the South as well.

ANTICOMMUNISM AND VIETNAM

In 1964 anticommunism was a strong Goldwater campaign theme, and generally speaking was an attitude closely shared by his early supporters. In 1968, however, this was not a particularly strong predictor of support for Wallace except among those who had graduated from high school or college. These middle-class (relatively speaking) Wallace backers were about 10 percentage points above the Nixon group and about 20 percentage points above Humphrey's supporters in their opposition to communism, as measured by the anticommunism index reported in Table V.19.

On the issue of Vietnam, however, we find some extreme differences between Wallace supporters and the remainder of the sample. Tables V.20 and V.21 present the positions of the candidate-preference groups on the question of initial involvement in the war in Vietnam and in the solutions they favored. Wallace backers were more than twice as likely as Humphrey's group to favor the most hawkish of the three alternatives, and almost 15 percentage points above the Nixon supporters on this measure. Like Goldwater's supporters in 1964, however, Wallace's backers were (by a slight margin) the group most hostile to initial involvement in the war.

AUTHORITARIANISM AND POLITICAL VIOLENCE

In the fall of 1968 I participated in the design of a national sample survey for the National Commission on the Causes and Prevention of Violence. The purpose of the survey (at least the portion of it with which I was concerned) was to isolate persons in the electorate who were disproportionately tolerant of or disposed toward the use of violence in politics. In order to do this, William A. Gamson and I developed a number of indices, derived from factor analyses, which attempted to measure approval or disapproval of police, military, political, and various other types of personal violence. These indices and the survey are described in detail in the commission's report.[11] Table V.22 presents the distribution, by level of education, of the candidate-preference groups on one of those measures, an index of verbal support for violent actions against political elites and extreme distrust of the government, which I have termed "political vengeance." At every educational level, Wallace supporters were *at least* twice as likely, and sometimes three or four times as likely, as the other candidate-

[11]National Commission of the Causes and Prevention of Violence, *Assassinations and Political Violence* (Washington, D.C.: U.S. Government Printing Office, 1969).

TABLE V.19

Scores of Candidate-Preference Groups on Anticommunism Index, by Educational Level, 1968

	Anticommunism Scores							
	Low		Medium		High		Total	
	N	%	N	%	N	%	N	%
LESS THAN 4 YEARS OF HIGH SCHOOL								
Wallace supporters	22	59.5%	12	32.4%	3	8.1%	37	100.0%
Humphrey supporters	78	65.5	38	31.9	3	2.5	119	100.0
Nixon supporters	43	61.4	19	27.1	8	11.4	70	100.0
Undecided and other	17	60.7	6	21.4	5	17.9	28	100.0
Total	160	63.0	75	29.5	19	7.5	254	100.0
HIGH SCHOOL GRADUATE OR SOME COLLEGE								
Wallace supporters	49	45.8	45	42.1	13	12.1	107	100.0
Humphrey supporters	171	65.0	87	33.1	5	1.9	263	100.0
Nixon supporters	187	53.7	138	39.7	23	6.6	348	100.0
Undecided and other	60	60.6	35	35.4	4	4.0	99	100.0
Total	467	57.2	305	37.3	45	5.5	817	100.0
COLLEGE GRADUATE OR MORE								
Wallace supporters	8	80.0	0	0.0	2	20.0	10	100.0
Humphrey supporters	37	75.5	11	22.4	1	2.0	49	100.0
Nixon supporters	70	68.0	26	25.2	7	6.8	103	100.0
Undecided and other	9	69.2	3	23.0	1	7.9	13	100.0
Total	124	73.2	40	17.6	11	9.2	175	100.0

TABLE V.20

Opinions of Candidate-Preference Groups on Involvement in Vietnam, 1968

	Did Right Thing by Becoming Involved		Other		Should Have Stayed Out		Don't Know		Total	
	N	%	N	%	N	%	N	%	N	%
Wallace supporters	44	28.6%	4	2.6%	88	57.1%	18	11.7%	154	100.0%
Humphrey supporters	147	34.0	4	0.9	211	48.8	70	16.3	432	100.0
Nixon supporters	158	30.4	7	1.3	291	56.0	63	12.3	519	100.0
Undecided and other	44	31.4	1	0.7	58	41.4	37	26.4	140	100.0
Total	393	31.4	16	1.3	648	51.8	188	15.0	1,245	100.0

TABLE V.21

Solutions to Vietnam Involvement Favored by Candidate-Preference Groups, 1968

	Pull Out Now		Remain, Try to End War		Take a Stronger Stand		Total	
	N	%	N	%	N	%	N	%
Wallace supporters	20	14.6%	32	23.4%	85	62.0%	137	100.0%
Humphrey supporters	91	23.0	189	47.8	115	29.1	395	100.0
Nixon supporters	98	20.5	200	41.9	179	37.5	477	100.0
Undecided and other	26	21.0	43	34.7	55	44.4	124	100.0
Total	235	20.7	464	41.0	434	38.3	1,133	100.0

preference groups to score at the extreme high end of the Political Vengeance Index. These people were very angry indeed with the government, and the recurring themes of violence in Wallace's campaign must have met with the approval of 30 to 50 percent of his supporters.

A second table (V.23) from the violence survey gives the distributions of the groups on a combined measure of anomy and authoritarianism, psychological traits that have often been assigned some explanatory importance in decomposing the causes of political extremism.

TABLE V.22

Scores of Candidate-Preference Groups on Political Vengeance, by Educational Level, 1968
(In Percentages)

	Political Vengeance Scores*					Total	
	Low	Lower Medium	Upper Medium	High		N	%
LESS THAN 4 YEARS OF HIGH SCHOOL							
Wallace supporters	11.1%	37.8%	20.0%	31.1%		48	100.0%
Humphrey supporters	23.1	43.6	21.4	12.0		120	100.0
Nixon supporters	20.2	41.6	29.2	9.0		92	100.0
Undecided and other	15.8	44.7	25.3	14.2		77	100.0
HIGH SCHOOL GRADUATE OR SOME COLLEGE							
Wallace supporters	10.5	59.6	15.8	22.6		57	100.0
Humphrey supporters	28.2	50.5	16.5	51.2		104	100.0
Nixon supporters	26.2	53.7	11.6	20.2		166	100.0
Undecided and other	22.6	51.2	8.5	6.0		84	100.0
COLLEGE GRADUATE OR MORE							
Wallace supporters	22.4	44.4	11.1	33.3		9	100.0
Humphrey supporters	37.0	44.4	18.5	44.4		27	100.0
Nixon supporters	31.2	54.2	10.4	16.7		48	100.0
Undecided and other	33.3	44.4	4.2	5.6		18	100.0

Source: National Commission on the Causes and Prevention of Violence, *Assassination and Political Violence* (Washington, D.C.: U.S. Government Printing Office, 1969).

*See Appendix for index items. Mean inter-item correlation = .238.

TABLE V.23

Scores of Candidate-Preference Groups on Anomic Authoritarianism,
by Educational Level, 1968
(In Percentages)

| | *Anomic Authoritarianism Scores** | | | *Total* | |
	Low	*Medium*	*High*	*N*	*%*
LESS THAN 4 YEARS OF **HIGH SCHOOL**					
Wallace supporters	8.9%	53.4%	37.8%	48	100.0%
Humphrey supporters	21.6	51.6	26.7	120	100.0
Nixon supporters	20.3	47.2	32.6	92	100.0
Undecided and other	20.6	46.0	33.4	77	100.0
HIGH SCHOOL GRADUATE OR **SOME COLLEGE**					
Wallace supporters	30.3	50.0	19.7	57	100.0
Humphrey supporters	52.0	39.2	8.9	104	100.0
Nixon supporters	36.0	50.3	13.7	166	100.0
Undecided and other	36.1	49.4	14.4	84	100.0
COLLEGE GRADUATE OR MORE					
Wallace supporters	44.4	33.3	22.2	9	100.0
Humphrey supporters	46.1	34.6	19.6	26	100.0
Nixon supporters	58.3	37.5	4.2	48	100.0
Undecided and other	55.6	44.5	0.0	18	100.0

Source: National Commission on the Causes and Prevention of Violence, *Assassination and Political Violence* (Washington, D.C.: U.S. Government Printing Office, 1969).
*The items in this index consist of three from the California F scale and three from McClosky and Scharr's Anomy Scale. They are reproduced in the Appendix.

In Chapter II we saw that there was some evidence that psychological (as opposed to political) authoritarianism or intolerance was positively associated with support for the late Senator Joseph McCarthy and for some of the groups making up the organized right in the United States. Wallace supporters also scored higher on this measure than the other groups at each level of education, but the differences were not pronounced. Often no more than 3 or 4 percentage points separated the Wallace group from the others. Thus psychological authoritarianism, while somewhat more prevalent among Wallace supporters than among the others, does not seem to be a very important discriminating variable in the sample from which these data were collected.

MODELS OF SUPPORT FOR WALLACE

The data that we have thus far reviewed point to a number of variables that differentiate Wallace supporters from the remainder of the electorate. Figures V.2 and V.3 are attempts to evaluate the arguments that I have put forward earlier concerning the origins of support for Wallace in the South and in the rest of the country. By placing the variables we have been discussing in a hypothetical causal sequence and introducing simultaneous controls through the use of dummy variable multiple regression,[12] I hope to provide a clear picture of the effects of the demographic and attitudinal variables that I have presumed are partially responsible for Wallace's support.

The model employs Betas, which provide a measure of the relative magnitude of the effect of a single variable when the effects of all other variables are held constant. It should be emphasized that the magnitude of a Beta is of no assistance in the placement of a variable in a causal sequence; this must be done on the basis of a more or less well-developed theory. The variables are arranged from left to right in the presumed chronological sequence of their emergence as factors in the development of an intention to vote for Wallace.

The variables in the model are often dummies (that is, they do not have a range of values beyond 0 and 1), and in the case of boxes with labels that refer to previously discussed indices, such as "Opposition to civil rights" and "Low legitimacy of political institutions," the single item most highly correlated with the total index was used as the variable in this multivariate model. This was done in order to reduce as much as possible the loss of cases from the model, because the greater the number of items in a variable, the greater the chance of encountering gaps in the data, therefore forcing that respondent out of the equations altogether.

The numbers in bold-face type are Betas; the others, enclosed in parentheses, are zero-order correlation coefficients indicating the relationship between that particular independent variable and the dependent variable without control for the other variables in the model. Let us examine the model in more detail.

[12]Multiple classification analysis, a form of dummy variable multiple regression, was used to compute Betas, or indicators of the relative importance of a variable in a joint explanation of the dependent variable. Betas are *not* the equivalent of partial correlation coefficients and, except in cases of wholly orthogonal variables, cannot be squared to produce a proportion of the variance explained by the set of predictors. The model assumes both linearity and the additivity of the variables. See F. M. Andrews, J. N. Morgan, and J. A. Sonquist, *Multiple Classification Analysis* (Ann Arbor: Institute for Social Research, University of Michigan, 1967).

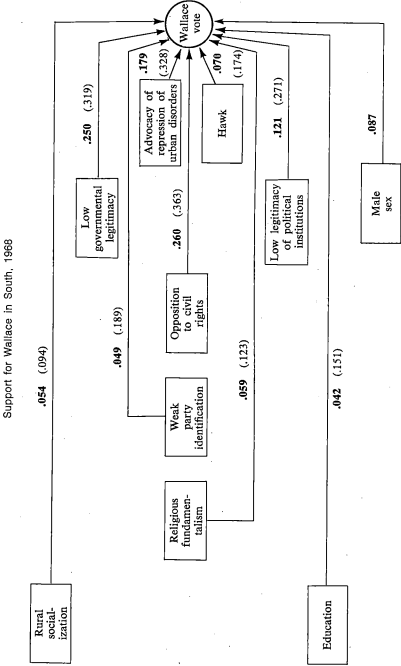

FIGURE V.2

Support for Wallace in South, 1968

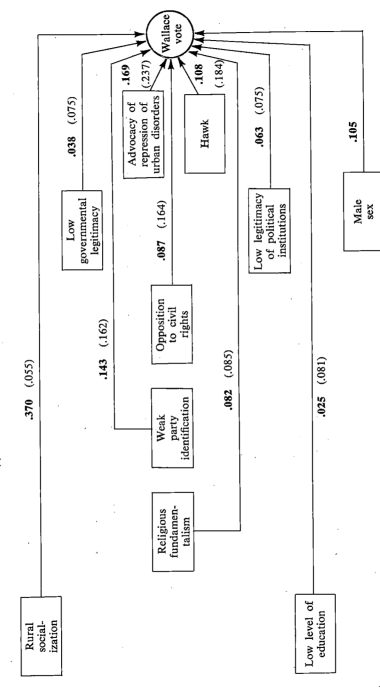

FIGURE V.3

Support for Wallace in North, West, and Midwest, 1968

The two variables at the extreme left of the model, rural socialization and low level of education, have a considerably stronger effect in the South than elsewhere. Indeed, outside of the South the independent effect of these variables is negligible. Presumably a rural background is more likely to produce fundamentalist religious beliefs, weak party identification, and the like. A low level of education, as we have seen, has a rather strong effect on the distributions of Wallace supporters over various attitudinal variables, some of which appear later in the model.

With respect to the placement of the remaining variables, I argue as follows: In the South, opposition to civil rights is part of the culture and developed prior to a decline in belief in the legitimacy of the government and of political institutions. Presumably these attitudes, while latent in many southerners, were not strongly activated at the mass level until the emergence of the civil rights movement in the late fifties and the eventual support given it by the federal government. Perhaps, though, Strom Thurmond's campaign in 1948 is a better event from which to date the emergence of modern political opposition to the federal government by white southerners exercised over the issue of civil rights.

Finally, the attitudes and policy preferences indicated in the variables at the right of the model must certainly have developed only recently, with the war in Vietnam and the occurrence of widespread urban rioting. There is an independent effect of male sex in each version of the model.

In the South, the strongest predictor of support for Wallace is, as we would expect, direct opposition to civil rights for Negroes. Following this is disbelief in governmental legitimacy and then the advocacy of the use of maximum force in quelling urban disorders. The effect of weak party identification in the South is comparatively slight ($\beta = .049$). Deviation from major party presidential tickets by southern racists is now the rule rather than the exception.

Outside the South, we have a rather different pattern. Here advocacy of the repression of urban disorders is the strongest predictor of support for Wallace. But note that the influence of direct opposition to civil rights is not nearly so great as it was in the South. Weak party identification ($\beta = .143$) is an important component of Wallace support outside the South, as is holding a hawkish position on Vietnam policy. It is interesting, but not too surprising, that the effect of the legitimacy variables is much weaker in the North, West, and Midwest than it is in the South. Clearly the federal government has not yet angered people in those regions to the degree that it has in the South.

I conceive of northern support for Wallace as developing along these lines: Religious fundamentalism, slightly affected by rural socialization, suggests a generally provincial outlook on the part of Wallace supporters in the North. This in turn led to rather low levels of party identification. Great concern over urban riots and to a somewhat lesser extent a hawkish position on Vietnam, accompanied by some direct opposition to civil rights for Negroes—all issues that Wallace has confronted with more overt belligerence than any recent administration— have led a number of northerners to prefer Wallace.

WALLACE AND RELATIVE DEPRIVATION

While there is probably much empirical research presently being done on Wallace, I am aware of only one study that has examined support for him from a rather different perspective than the one I have taken here. This study, by Robert Riley and Thomas Pettigrew,[13] is based on a number of sample surveys in northern urban areas. Riley and Pettigrew describe their samples of Wallace supporters as experiencing *relative deprivation;* specifically, white workers who supported Wallace felt that blacks were "getting ahead too fast" and that, relative to themselves, were advancing in society more rapidly than their abilities or efforts warranted. Such feelings, Riley and Pettigrew argue, are likely to produce support for Wallace. I believe this is an important theoretical finding, and I look forward to the publication of their analysis.

CONCLUSION

Generally speaking, the data indicate that those who supported George Wallace in the presidential election of 1968 were immediately motivated by threats they perceive to originate from blacks. In the South, much of Wallace's support was based on simple opposition to civil rights; in other parts of the country the primary motivation was probably fear of blacks and the desire to repress any further rioting by them. The marginal-participant theory, tested in the form of strength of party identification, received some limited confirmation in the North, but I have noted that the measures used to test this theory must be interpreted cautiously.

[13]Robert T. Riley and Thomas F. Pettigrew, "Relative Deprivation and Wallace's Northern Support" (a paper presented at the annual meeting of the American Sociological Association, San Francisco, September 2, 1969).

CHAPTER VI

The Social Origins of
Contemporary Rightist Movements:
A Theoretical View[1]

WHEN MAJOR SOCIAL CHANGE occurs in any society, value conflicts of a profound and inevitably political character follow. Accompanying those changes we term "modern"—large-scale technological development and industrialization, rural-to-urban population shifts, and the like—has been the formation of social groups that are differentially affected by these changes and which are supported and motivated by the dominant values in the social system, on the one hand, and on the other by the potential values made possible by the unsettled circumstances brought about by change. Under such conditions, some groups are likely to move up and others down in both the economic and the prestige orders of the society. Common distinctions between these two groups are often suggested by phrases like "haves and have-nots" and "radicals and conservatives." Such catchwords often guide our thinking away from the prestige-related aspects of group formation and action and direct our attention to the relative *economic* power of groups rather than toward the degree to which political action among those affected segments of the population is motivated by *values* and *symbols,* which are of central importance in the maintenance of a group's *prestige.*

Nowhere has the importance of symbolic issues as the motivational basis for action in American protest politics been more succinctly

[1]I wish to thank Professor Leon Mayhew for his valuable counsel and assistance in the preparation of this chapter.

expressed than in Joseph Gusfield's excellent study of the temperance movement, *Symbolic Crusade*.[2] My own analysis of the Goldwater and Wallace movements has taken a course parallel to Gusfield's, and I have developed a reasonably congruent set of descriptive and explanatory ideas about the genesis of symbolic or, as Gusfield calls them, "status" movements; but his analysis has been most useful to my formulation of these conclusions.

Gusfield's analysis of the temperance movement is based on a conception of status politics which is very different from the theories of status discrepancy based on mismatched components of stratification, which we have seen to have so little utility in the explanation of either the Wallace or the Goldwater phenomenon, or of the radical right. Gusfield says that when status groups

vie with each other to change or defend their prestige allocation, they do so through symbolic rather than instrumental goals. The significant meanings are not given in the intrinsic properties of the action but *in what it has come to signify for the participants*. It is symbolic in the sense that we speak of the cross as the symbol of Christianity, of pens as phallic symbols, and of clothing and styles as symbols of social status. In symbolic behavior the action is ritualistic and ceremonial in that the goal is reached in the behavior itself rather than in any state which it brings about.[3]

This distinction between symbolic and instrumental action can also be expressed as a difference between *community-oriented action,* or action that functions to enhance group solidarity, and *class-oriented action,* which serves to protect the economic integrity of a group.

Gusfield's formulation of the concept of status politics emphasizes the relative decline of social groups with respect to their roles as advocates and followers of once dominant values in the society rather than objective discrepancy in socioeconomic status among individuals, which is the basis for much of previous status-discrepancy theory.

The relevance of these ideas here is that, in my judgment, the Goldwater and Wallace movements were symbolic political movements, and those who participated in them were motivated largely by *expressive* rather than instrumental needs. This is an important distinction, because, as we shall see, it places analytic emphasis upon two sociological concepts, the moral order and the stratification system, each of which is an important determinant of group and individual action, but is not necessarily directly or perfectly linked with the place of the group in the economic order.

[2]Joseph Gusfield, *Symbolic Crusade* (Urbana: University of Illinois Press, 1963).
[3]*Ibid.,* p. 21 (my italics).

Groups[4] in a society are sustained by economic integrity, by internal reinforcement of group-specific norms and values, and by external social support for these norms and values from other groups in the society. External social support may also be termed legitimacy, for it occurs when another group or the public at large recognizes the validity of the values that legitimize the lives and contributions of a status group. All groups established in a society share a subset of values ("common values") but deviate from each other in their economic or class locations and, among other things, in the specific norms, customs, and beliefs that help to form their distinctive life styles. Groups vary in the degree to which they receive external social support for these distinctive patterns. And in this sense they differ in the degree of their participation in the moral order, for the morality of a group, sociologically speaking, varies directly with its degree of acceptance within the total society. We all know, for example, that the enforcement of moral conformity (i.e., resocialization) by the dominant groups in American culture was much more intensive with eastern European immigrants to this country than it was with northern Europeans.[5]

The important point is that once a group is established in the economic order, possesses mechanisms of internal reinforcement of its norms, and receives external social support, the *prestige* of that group's members becomes dependent upon the maintenance of these conditions. Economic decline, challenges to the group-specific normative system, and withdrawal of social support are, singly or together, direct threats to the prestige of that group. My analysis of the Wallace and Goldwater movements is based upon my observation that the latter event—the withdrawal of social support—is responsible for the formation of the symbolic political movements that coalesced around these two presidential candidates.

---

[4]By "groups" I mean aggregates of persons who share relatively equal levels of authority, and are united by a manifest or latent (in which case a group is a potential or quasi group) characteristic that at the minimum must include a feeling of belongingness, or at least have the potential for the development of such feelings. (See Ralf Dahrendorf, *Class and Class Conflict in Industrial Society* [Stanford, Calif.: Stanford University Press, 1959], pp. 179–93.) Groups are often given form by their coalescence around political candidates who express the interests of the group "as interests related to the legitimacy of relations of domination and subjection" (*ibid.,* p. 181). Wallace and Goldwater supporters are groups that have common interests in exactly this sense, as my argument here will, I hope, demonstrate.

[5]It is important to note also that integration of a group can be *prevented* if the dominant groups in a society control its environment so thoroughly that a caste position can be ascribed to all of the group's members. The obvious case is the American Negro.

These movements (and others like them) occur because of the fact that social change, by challenging the established order of values, induces shifts in the prestige order of a society, and prestige is a valued social and psychological attribute to be defended by groups and persons threatened with its loss.

When economic disorder and decline threaten a group with established prestige, we often call this group's political response a class movement. When the normative components of an established group's claim to recognition and prestige are threatened, the response is often a movement directed primarily at affirmation of the social importance of the group's normative patterns. These Gusfield has termed status movements. Thus we find movements of the type centering on Goldwater and Wallace, largely concerned with the implementation of policies and the reaffirmation of the values and norms that once established the dissenting group's importance in the prestige order of the society. In the case of the Goldwater movement, for example, we see affirmation of the norms of individual effort and entrepreneurial activity for their own sake—both norms that are perceived as (and may in fact be) severely challenged by the present economic and technological structures of American society. In the Wallace movement, we see racism as a desire to maintain an increasingly threatened traditional status-deference pattern upon which southerners and the white urban working classes have depended as one important component of their prestige for many, many years. One description of the function of this pattern is found in Morison's discussion of the "fecund 1890s":

The real motive of jim crow laws was to keep the Negro down and make him constantly sensible of his inferior status. That is why jim crow policy had so irresistible an appeal to the poor whites. Except for the "hillbillies," who lived apart and fairly respectably, these lower-class whites of the South were a very unfortunate people—poor, illiterate, and diseased; but their feeling that the poorer of them was superior to even the most cultured Negro flattered their ego and assuaged their griefs.[6]

The process through which groups undergo a loss of prestige I term "transitional unrepresentation." This notion is based upon a dynamic conception of the prestige order and in some respects is derived from pluralist theory. That is, classes and groups form in a society and have three distinct (but not mutually exclusive) phases of relations with the norms and formal political structures of that society. In their initial phase, as challenging groups (recent historical examples are organized

[6]Samuel Eliot Morison, *The Oxford History of the American People* (New York: Oxford University Press, 1965), pp. 792–93.

labor and American Negroes), they seek admission to the political and prestige orders of the society through the use of a combination of symbolic and instrumental actions, largely (in the United States) directed at appeals to "democratic principles," and through rapid socialization of members into the common values of the society. When they reach the stage of representation, they are accorded *potentially* equal access to the legal, economic, and prestige orders of the society. Finally, a group may begin a process of withdrawal from representation—or transitional unrepresentation—when economic, technological, environmental, or normative changes undermine the economic or normative structures upon which the affected group depends. Two major historical examples of this process have been cited, the decline of the small entrepreneur and decreasing social support for prestige-dependent racists; and there have been others. The increasing secularization of churches and the development of the social gospel, for instance, threaten the stability and prestige of fundamentalist religious groups.[7]

Relative deprivation—a condition that, as I mentioned above, Riley and Pettigrew found to be most significantly associated with support for Wallace in the northern urban areas they surveyed[8]—is the *economic* corollary of transitional unrepresentation. Relative deprivation has most often been thought of as primarily a social process and psychological state disproportionately present in *challenging groups*. But there is no good reason to confine it to insurgent strata, and it seems equally applicable to declining groups if the concept is defined as a feeling of relatively lower rewards from the economic (and sociopolitical) system than those obtained by other visible social groups. Such a feeling is clearly part of the complex of attitudes held by the members of both the Goldwater and the Wallace movements, and are, as Riley and Pettigrew found, particularly important as sources of support for Wallace.

Despite the analytic utility of these distinctions among challenging, represented, and unrepresented groups, it is probably most useful to think of these stages as conditions of greater or lesser representation rather than as wholly disjunctive states. Even though a group may be represented, it may be less well represented than others. It is probably useful to think of groups as arrayed along a dimension of security, from high to low. Security is a composite variable composed of the three components of group status I mentioned earlier: economic integ-

---

[7]These terms and the conceptions of pluralism discussed here derive from research now in process by William A. Gamson, in which I participated in 1967–1968.
[8]Robert T. Riley and Thomas F. Pettigrew, "Relative Deprivation and Wallace's Northern Support" (a paper presented at the annual meeting of the American Sociological Association, San Francisco, September 2, 1969).

rity, internal cohesion, and social support or legitimacy. Groups that enjoy great security in this sense are in my view not likely to participate in symbolic politics; groups less secure are more likely to participate in this kind of political action. From this it follows that groups *advancing or declining* in social prestige, economic security, and the like are those from which symbolic political movements are to be expected. The Wallace group in 1968 and the Goldwater group in 1964 seem to me to have been responding to a loss of group security, but there are historical examples, especially in the nativist movements discussed below, in which symbolic politics functioned further to integrate partially represented groups into the dominant social order. That is, symbolic politics are the politics of groups that enjoy relatively greater repre-sentation than newly challenging groups but which are somewhat marginal with respect to their relations with the dominant segments of the society. In the case of declining groups, the target of their hostility and criticism is the society at large. In the case of advancing groups, other, less represented groups have often served as scapegoats whose rejection and chastisement by a symbolic movement serves the purpose of confirming the moral worth and correctness of the advancing but not yet wholly accepted group.

It is here that the extent of a group's participation in the moral order becomes an important analytic variable. Symbolic politics, as I have said earlier, are directed at affirmation of one source of a group's integrity, social support. The content of symbolic political actions is largely directed at affirmation of the moral worth of the group and is an effort to secure or regain social support. We have seen in the Wallace and Goldwater movements two examples of this process of moral affirmation under conditions of declining support. It should not be overlooked that a major component of these groups' claims to moral rectitude is based on their *condemnation* of the moral basis of the dominant segments of the society. It should also be clear that *affirmation* of the dominant group's morality can serve as a powerful basis for symbolic politics as well.

The Ku Klux Klan in the twentieth century, for example, is an organization that seems to fit this pattern quite well. Dedicated to the rigid enforcement of a code of fundamentalist morality as well as suppression of blacks, Ku Kluxers may well have acted to demonstrate their worthiness of advancement to full representation in southern society. By repressing deviants and being letter-perfect in their adherence to certain visible aspects of public morality, Klansmen may' have believed that they garnered the approval of their better represented fellows. If so, their actions would correctly be seen as efforts to acquire social support for the groups disproportionately represented in the Klan's following. The Klan, sociologically speaking, has served the same function as another agency of social control, the militant Sunday school; only in their means of implementation do they differ.

The reasons that the Goldwater and Wallace movements become national at this time, rather than at some earlier period, are complicated.[9] Briefly, I believe that challenges to a group's prestige in the form of withdrawal of external social support bring the group into a specifically *political* national arena only after the historical process of transitional unrepresentation has advanced so far that the danger to the group of the challenges to its values can no longer go unrecognized. At this point mobilization of the group's members becomes possible because of the increasing visibility of the challenge. Thus the normative legitimacy that was once granted a status group by reason of its representation within the pluralist power and value matrix is replaced by an effort to reestablish, *through formal political processes,* the social support for the group's norms and values which has permanently or temporarily disappeared.

It may be useful at this point to consider some of the historical origins of rightist social movements in the United States. I criticized the late Professor Schlesinger[10] for his identification of the Goldwater movement as an example of a historical tradition of extremism dating from the American Protective Association and the Know-Nothings. As I tried to show in Chapters III and IV, the supposed extremism of the Goldwater movement was largely a myth. Nevertheless, the class of historical social movements to which the Goldwater and Wallace movements seem to be most closely related is, in fact, the nativist movements. These national political movements began to appear in the United States after the 1840s. The first of these, the Native American party, an agglomeration of "no popery" Republicans and other anti-Catholic groups, held its first national convention on July 4, 1845, declaring its opposition to Catholics and foreigners and establishing a platform that included what was to become by the end of the century the prime policy goal of nativist groups: the restriction of immigration.[11] Other nativist movements that reached into national politics included the Know-Nothing (or American) party, which flourished in the latter

[9]Many attempts to introduce into national politics the policies advocated by the Wallace and Goldwater movements have occurred in the past thirty years. See the Preface for remarks about some of these efforts.

[10]Arthur M. Schlesinger, Sr., "Extremism in American Politics," *Saturday Review,* November 27, 1965, pp. 21–25.

[11]Ray Allen Billington, *The Protestant Crusade, 1800–1860* (Chicago: Quadrangle Books, 1964), pp. 193–219.

half of the decade preceding the Civil War. The party sent forty-three representatives to the Thirty-fourth Congress, controlled a number of state legislatures, and attained a quarter of the popular vote in the national election of 1856 (their candidate was former president Millard Fillmore). The American Protective Association (APA) emerged as an important political force in the 1890s. Like the Native American and Know-Nothing parties, this group was national in scope, anti-Catholic, and antiforeign.[12] Nativism and nativist groups continued to appear and have political importance throughout the first thirty years of the twentieth century.

Neither the Wallace nor especially the Goldwater movement was as *overtly* bigoted and antidemocratic or extremist as the Native American party or many of its successors; both recent movements appear to have conformed more closely to the American common value of political tolerance than the earlier movements did.

I nevertheless suggest that the social forces that stimulated the growth of the nativist parties are in many ways comparable to those that produced the Goldwater and Wallace movements. One similarity among all these movements is found in the fact that they appear to be status movements largely formed in response to intrusive challenges to the normative patterns of established groups. Their appearance is a manifestation of pattern-maintenance behavior; their participants, drawn from differentially affected segments of the society, are responding to perceived threats to their prestige on the one hand, and on the other to a need for further acceptance into the moral, economic, and political orders of society.

The Wallace and Goldwater movements, like some of the earlier nativist movements, differ rather strikingly from each other in their *class* base and therefore in the degree of their commitment to procedural norms, and to some extent in the policies advocated by their leaders and desired by their members. But as we have seen, these two groups share a common opposition to social welfare liberalism and civil rights for Negroes, while also expressing relatively greater hostility to other minority groups, especially Catholics and Jews, than the remainder of the population. Furthermore, both groups express strong approval of militarism, at least insofar as they support highly aggressive policies in Vietnam and oppose American negotiations with hostile "communist" nations. From the sociological perspective I am applying here, they are also most significantly alike by reason of the fact that their views on these issues are *vastly* at odds with those held by much of the popula-

[12]*Ibid.*, pp. 380–436, and John Higham, *Strangers in the Land: Patterns of American Nativism, 1860–1925* (New York: Atheneum, 1963), pp. 4–56.

tion of the United States during the years in which these survey data were collected. This empirical fact underlines the importance of the problem of external recognition of the ideologies by which status groups live. Indeed, the *covert* character of the racism of the Wallace movement in particular—at least outside of Alabama—is an indication of a massive shift in the norms of the society during the past hundred years. Moreover, to restate the obvious, the areas of social and political policy about which the followers of Goldwater and Wallace become most exercised are precisely those that have involved the greatest redirection of values and social policy on the part of both the American public and the governing elite in the last thirty years, and therefore would presumably have the greatest impact on groups whose prestige depended on the maintenance of earlier patterns and policies.

Before closing this discussion of historical antecedents of these movements, let us consider some of the causal factors that historians have isolated as responsible for the appearance of previous nativist movements in American history. Although historical theories of causation are somewhat limited, both economic- and status-related variables have been used (singly or together) as explanations of various movements of the past. As we have seen, the theory of agrarian political behavior developed in *The American Voter*[13] relies heavily on the assumption of extreme economic sensitivity of that segment of the electorate eventually mobilized into support of third parties; this explanation seems to have some application to the previous nativist movements (some of which emerged as third parties) as well. John Higham, for example, argues that economic depression, external foreign threats, and the kinds of normative disruptions brought about by urbanization and the development of large-scale industrial work forces in the presence of extensive, culturally heterogeneous in-migration largely from eastern and southern Europe were responsible for much of the nativism, nationalism, and 100 percent Americanism that periodically raged across the country through the nineteenth and early twentieth centuries.[14] These factors, according to Higham, worked sometimes together and sometimes alone to spur or flag the nativist impulse.

Nativist movements, in Higham's view, are divisible into three distinct types whose formal ideologies and mass appeals stem from the intellectual traditions of anti-Catholicism, racism, and anti(left-wing)-radicalism. Higham argues that the oldest and most powerful of these traditions in the earlier periods was anti-Catholicism, with racism and

[13]Angus Campbell *et al., The American Voter* (New York: Wiley, 1960), chap. 15.
[14]Higham, *Strangers in the Land.*

antiradicalism slowly emerging as the dominant patterns in the 1890s. And antiradicalism and racism are still the major themes of conservative and rightist protest in the United States. Although we do not have exactly comparable data for the 1964 and 1968 elections, it is clear that racism played a strong part in the Wallace vote, and to some extent in the Goldwater vote. Moreover, there is no question that antiradicalism was not only a strong predictor of support for Wallace, but an important theme in Goldwater's campaign as well. Thus there appears to be a strong thread of continuity between the Wallace and Goldwater movements and the later nativist movements in the content of the symbolic issues that drew the groups together. Also, of course, the nativist movements and those led by Goldwater and Wallace share an intense nationalism, patriotism (often chauvinism), and a high degree of expressive and ritualistic "Americanism"—all forms of socially integrative behavior described by Katz, Kelman, and Flacks as examples of "symbolic integration."[15]

The origins of the intense nationalism of these groups is found in the fact that they identify their life styles and locations in the prestige order with a mythical (although partially historically based) concept of the state. Thus, while the contemporary state has been a prime agent of the disruption of the prestige order of American society, these groups invoke in their defense a concept of the state based upon a reactionary view of history and harken back to a time when the state represented the values they hold dear and positively sanctioned the norms they admire. The function of this invocation is obvious: it is an effort to bolster declining prestige by creating a direct identification of the affected group with the most powerful formal political structure in the society—the state.

It will soon be possible, through the use of historical and third-party data (now being prepared for computer processing by the Survey Research Center at the University of Michigan), to test these ideas more carefully. Until then, I offer this analysis simply as a rough hypothesis, badly in need of further operationalization and empirical verification, in the hope that it may clarify some of the forces in American society that produce social movements of a conservative and sometimes antidemocratic character.

[15]Daniel Katz, Herbert Kelman, and Richard Flacks, "The National Role: Some Hypotheses About the Relations of Individuals to the Nation in America Today" (a paper presented at the Peace Research Conference, University of Chicago, November 1963).

APPENDIX

ANALYTIC GROUPS

BOTH THE GOLDWATER and the Wallace groups in this analysis consisted of respondents who expressed the intention of voting for their group's candidate—Goldwater in 1964 or Wallace in 1968. In the case of the Goldwater group, vote intention was combined with a preconvention preference for the senator. No such test could be used with the Wallace supporters. While it would have been possible to try to eliminate dropouts by checking a respondent's reported vote (in the postelection study) against his preelection candidate preference, both the 1964 and 1968 studies have shown that the reported vote measure is not very reliable. Many people who obviously voted for Goldwater reported that they did not vote or voted for Johnson, and the same pattern appears to have occurred among Wallace supporters.

A question not covered in this volume is the great drop in support for Wallace during the thirty-day period prior to the election. I made an attempt to examine respondents who expressed an intention of voting for Wallace and then after the election reported that they had actually voted for either Humphrey or Nixon; but because of the very small number of cases and the problems inherent in reports of voting, I abandoned this analysis. One point that might be worth noting, however, is the fact that those persons who did report shifting from Wallace to other candidates had, if anything, *weaker* party identifications than those reporting that they had stayed with him through the election.

INDEX ITEMS AND INTERITEM CORRELATIONS
FROM THE 1964 ELECTION STUDY,
SURVEY RESEARCH CENTER, UNIVERSITY OF MICHIGAN

(Not including the indices developed by the SRC; information on those scales is available in the 1964 codebooks.)

Anticommunism

1. Some people say that our farmers and businessmen should be able to go ahead and do business with Communist countries as long as the goods are not used for military purposes. Others say that our government should not allow Americans to trade with the Communist countries. Have you been interested enough in this to favor one side over the other? (Deck 12, Column 18, page 4)
2. Do you think Communist China should be admitted to the United Nations, or do you think it should not? (Deck 12; Column 24, page 7)
3. Some people feel that we must do something to get the Communist government out of Cuba. Others feel that it is up to the Cuban people to handle their own affairs. Have you been interested enough in this matter to favor one side over the other? (Deck 12, Column 26, page 8)

Mean inter-item correlation (Pearson's r) = .442.

Legitimacy of Government

1. Do you think quite a few of the people running the government are a little crooked, not very many are, or do you think hardly any of them are crooked at all? (Deck 13, Column 40, page 8)
2. Do you think that people in the government waste a lot of money we pay in taxes, waste some of it, or don't waste very much of it? (Deck 13, Column 41, page 8)
3. How much of the time do you think you can trust the government in Washington to do what is right—just about always, most of the time, or only some of the time? (Deck 13, Column 42, page 9)
4. Do you feel that almost all of the people running the government are smart people who usually know what they are doing, or do you think that quite a few of them don't seem to know what they are doing? (Deck 13, Column 43, page 9)
5. Would you say the government is pretty much run by a few big

interests looking out for themselves or that it is run for the benefit of all the people? (Deck 13, Column 44, page 9)

Mean inter-item correlation = .463.

Political Activism

1. Did you do any work for one of the parties or candidates? (Deck 11, Column 34, page 17)
2. Do you belong to any political club or organization? (Deck 11, Column 35, page 17)
3. Have you ever written to any public officials giving them your opinion about something that should be done? (Deck 11, Column 37, page 17)
4. Have you ever written a letter to the editor of a newspaper or magazine giving any political opinions? (Deck 11, Column 42, page 19)
5. Some people don't pay too much attention to election campaigns. How about you—were you very interested in this campaign, fairly interested, just slightly interested, or not interested at all in it? (Deck 11, Column 45, page 20)
6. Some people seem to think about what's going on in government all the time whether there's an election going on or not. Others aren't that interested. Would you say you follow what's going on in government? (Deck 11, Column 45, page 20)

Mean inter-item correlation = .529.

NEW INDEX ITEMS AND INTERITEM CORRELATIONS FROM THE 1968 ELECTION STUDY, SURVEY RESEARCH CENTER, UNIVERSITY OF MICHIGAN

Civil Rights Index

1. Some people feel that if Negroes are not getting fair treatment in jobs the government in Washington should see to it that they do. Others feel that this is not the federal government's business. Have you had enough interest in this question to favor one side over the other? If yes,
   (1) See to it that Negroes get fair treatment.

(3) Other.

(5) Leave these matters to local communities. (Variable #0073)

2. Some people say that the government in Washington should see to it that white and Negro children are allowed to go to the same schools. (Same probe as above.)

(1) Yes.

(3) Other.

(5) No.

(This item was used in the Multiple Clarification Analysis [MCA] model for civil rights.) (Variable #0075)

3. As you may know, Congress passed a bill that says that Negroes should have the right to go to any hotel or restaurant they can afford, just like anybody else. (Same probes and responses as above.) (Variable #0078)

4. Some say that the civil rights people have been trying to push too fast. Others feel that they haven't pushed fast enough. How about you?

(1) Too fast.

(3) About right.

(5) Too slowly. (Variable #0081)

5. During the past year or so, would you say that most of the actions Negroes have taken to get the things they want have been violent, or have most of these actions been peaceful?

(1) Most have been violent.

(2) More violent than peaceful.

(3) Some violent, some peaceful.

(4) More peaceful than violent.

(5) Most have been peaceful. (Variable #0082)

6. Which of these statements would you agree with?

(1) White people have a right to keep Negroes out of their neighborhoods if they want to.

(5) Negroes have a right to live wherever they can afford to, just like anybody else.

(8) Don't know. (Variable #0085)

7. Are you in favor of desegregation, strict segregation, or something in between?

(1) Desegregation.

(3) In between.

(5) Segregation. (Variable #0088)

Mean inter-item correlation = .389.

Political Attention Index

1. Some people seem to follow what's going on in government and public affairs most of the time, whether there's an election going on or not. Others aren't that interested. Would you say you follow what's going on in government and public affairs most of the time, some of the time, only now and then, or hardly at all?
   (1) Most of the time.
   (2) Some of the time.
   (3) Only now and then.
   (4) Hardly at all. (Variable #0430)
2. First, how about international and world affairs; do you pay a great deal of attention, some attention, or not much attention to international affairs?
   (1) Great deal of attention.
   (3) Some.
   (5) Not much. (Variable #0431)
3. What about national affairs; do you pay a great deal, some, or not much attention to national affairs?
   (1) Great deal of attention.
   (3) Some.
   (5) Not much. (Variable #0432)
4. And how about affairs here in (STATE WHERE RESPONDENT LIVES); do you pay a great deal, some, or not much attention to state affairs?
   (1) Great deal of attention.
   (3) Some.
   (5) Not much. (Variable #0433)
5. Finally, what about local affairs; do you pay a great deal, some, or not much attention to local affairs?
   (1) Great deal of attention.
   (3) Some.
   (5) Not much. (Variable #0434)

Mean inter-item correlation = .267.

Political Efficacy Index

1. Would you say that most public officials care quite a lot about what people like you think, or that they don't care much at all?
   (1) Care.
   (5) Don't care. (Variable #0141)

2. Would you say that voting is the only way that people like you can have any say about the way the government runs things, or that there are lots of ways that you can have a say?
   (1) Lots of ways.
   (5) Voting only way.
   (6) No way to have a say. (Variable #0142)
3. Would you say that politics and government are so complicated that people like you can't really understand what's going on, or that you can understand what's going on pretty well?
   (1) Can understand.
   (5) Can't understand. (Variable #0143) ,
4. Would you say that people like you have quite a lot of say about what the government does, or that you don't have much say at all?
   (1) Have a lot to say.
   (5) Don't have much to say. (Variable #0144)

Mean inter-item correlation = .261.

Legitimacy of Government Index

1. Do you think that people in the government waste a lot of the money we pay in taxes, waste some of it, or don't waste very much of it?
   (1) Not much.
   (3) Some.
   (5) A lot. (Variable #0503)
2. How much of the time do you think that you can trust the government in Washington to do what is right—just about always, most of the time, or only some of the time?
   (1) Always.
   (2) Most of the time.
   (3) Some of the time.
   (5) None of the time. (Variable #0504)
3. Would you say the government is pretty much run by a few big interests looking out for themselves or that it is run for the benefit of all the people?
   (1) For the benefit of all.
   (5) Few big interests.
   (7) Other: depends; both boxes checked; refused to choose. (Variable #0505)
4. Do you feel that almost all of the people running the government are smart people who usually know what they are doing, or do you

think that quite a lot of them don't seem to know what they
are doing?

(1) Know what they're doing.

(5) Don't know what they're doing.

(7) Other: depends; both boxes checked; refused to choose. (Variable #0506)

5 Do you think that quite a few of the people running the government
are a little crooked, not very many are, or do you think hardly any
of them are crooked at all?

(1) Hardly any.

(3) Not many.

(5) Quite a lot. (Variable #0507)

Mean inter-item correlation = .296.

Anomic Authoritarianism

1. A few strong leaders could make this country better than all the
laws and the talk. (F scale)
2. People were better off in the old days when everyone knew just
how he was expected to act. (A scale)
3. Justice may have been a little rough and ready in the days of the
old West, but things worked better than they do today with all the
legal red tape.
4. What is lacking in the world today is the old kind of friendship
that lasted for a lifetime. (A scale)
5. Everything changes so quickly these days that I often have trouble
deciding which are the right rules to follow. (A scale)
6. What young people need most of all is strong discipline by their
parents. (F scale)

Mean inter-item correlation = .271.

Political Vengeance

1. Sometimes I have felt that the best thing for our country might be
the death of some of our political leaders.
2. Some politicians who have had their lives threatened probably
deserve it.
3. The government in Washington is the enemy, not the friend, of
people like me.

Mean inter-item correlation = .238.

INDEX

PRINTED IN U.S.A.

James McEvoy III holds a Ph.D. degree
from the University of Michigan, where
he has engaged in research at the Center
for Research on Conflict Resolution and
was assistant project director for studies
conducted by the Institute for Social Research on Utilization of Scientific Knowledge. He has also served as special
consultant and task force project director
for research on political violence for the
National Commission on the Causes and
Prevention of Violence. Currently assistant professor at the University of California, Davis, he has made numerous
contributions to scholarly journals and
edited volumes, and is himself the editor
of two well-received volumes on American political conflict.